# THE NUTT WACKIEST FUNNIEST SKITS EVER!

## by Stanley Snickelfoose

**PB**

Piccadilly Books, Ltd.
Colorado Springs, CO

Illustrations by Valerie Rivera

**Piccadilly Books, Ltd.**
**P.O. Box 25203**
**Colorado Springs, CO 80936, USA**
**www.piccadillybooks.com**
**info@piccadillybooks.com**

Library of Congress Cataloging-in-Publication Data

Snickelfoose, Stanley.
  The nuttiest, wackiest, funniest skits ever / by Stanley Snickelfoose.
     p. cm.
   ISBN 978-0-941599-68-9
  1. Comedy sketches. 2. Amateur plays. I. Title.
   PS3619.N529N88 2008
812'.6--dc22
                                              2008035838


Printed in the USA

# Table of Contents

# Introduction

In this book you will find some of the funniest, wackiest skits ever. Most use dialog, but a few are done in pantomime. All of the skits should be performed with wide, open movements and exaggerated gestures so the audience can see what is going on and to give the performance character and added humor.

The skits range in length from about 10 minutes to 1 minute. There are several short 1-2 minute skits that rely on only one or two bits of humor and end with the biggest laugh. The skits in this book, for the most part, are changeable or adaptable. You can change names and gender and even the dialog to suit your needs and preferences. You don't need to following them word for word, feel free to modify them to fit your personality and your situation. You may also add appropriate sound effects to the skits to enhance the humor and fun. The skits are designed for two or more participants. In many cases, however, the number of participants can vary. A perfect example of this is the skit titled "The Radio." In this skit only four participants are needed, but two, three, four or more players can easily be added. In fact, additional participants would make it more entertaining and enjoyable.

Many of these skits are new and original, others are based on classic skits that have thrilled audiences for years. All of the classic skits have been updated where necessary, sometimes the action has been modified and new dialog and jokes added to enhance their audience appeal.

The primary key in making these skits successful is to practice, practice, and practice. Put feeling into your voice and your actions.

Make the situation to appear to be real. Memorize the dialog, if any, and rehearse each step so that your timing is right on. Jokes and actions should be delivered as indicated. If your timing is off, it can weaken the punch line or slow down the action. A quick pace keeps the audience interested and entertained. You don't have the luxury of thinking about your next line or what your next action will be, it should be rehearsed well enough to come automatically and spontaneously. If you do these things, your performance will be a hit with the audience.

# The Animal Act

**Number of Participants:** Four or five

**Characters**: Jeff, Milo, Waiter, Businessman, Frog (the voice of the frog can come from Milo using ventriloquism or from someone offstage)

**Costumes:** Businessman is dressed in suit and tie. Waiter has apron on and dish towel over arm. Jeff and Milo wear street closes.

**Props:** Three chairs, two tables, newspaper, toy frog, and a fly (or something that can resemble a fly).

**Setting:** Two friends (Milo and Jeff) are sitting at a table in a restaurant. A businessman at a nearby table is reading a newspaper. Waiter is standing off to the side with a dish towel folded over his arm.

## The Performance

**Milo:** *(Speaking to Jeff)* I've discovered the most incredible animal act. I'll make a fortune and I want you to be my partner.

**Jeff:** Oh, yeah! Tell me about it?

**Milo:** *(Reaches into his pocket and pulls out a fly and holds it between his thumb and first finger. Fingers can move a little to show movement giving the fly animation and the appearance to being alive.)* This is my trained fly.

**Jeff:** *(Surprised)* Your what?

**Milo:** My trained fly. Watch. *(He puts the fly down in the center of the table.)* He obeys my every command. *(He looks at the fly and speaks in a commanding voice.)* Stay, stay boy. *(Looks back at Jeff)* See!

**Jeff:** That's amazing!

**Milo:** *(He pulls out a frog and holds it in his hand.)* There's more. Wait until you see the frog.

**Jeff:** Frog?

**Milo:** This is my frog. He is the other half of the act. You're really going to love this. *(Lifting the frog up)* Ask him what his name is?

**Jeff:** What? Ask your frog his name? Is he supposed to be a talking frog or something?

**Milo:** Yeah. Go ahead. Ask him.

**Jeff:** Ahh…what is your name little frog?

**Frog:** *(In a froggy voice)* Ree-bit!

**Milo:** Yes! His name is Ree-bit—Reebit the frog. Now ask him what would happen if he died.

**Jeff:** *(Skeptical)* What would happen if you died?

**Frog:** *(In frog-like voice)* Croak!

**Milo:** That's right. He would croak.

**Jeff:** Oh, this is ridiculous! That's the dumbest animal act I've ever seen. What are you going to do next—have him eat the fly?

**Businessman:** *(Leans toward Milo and Jeff, candidly listening to every word with great interest.)*

**Milo:** Wait that's not all. Ask him how old he is.

**Jeff:** What's he going to say fooor-ty. *(Imitating how a frog might say it.)*

**Frog:** For heavens sake no, I'm only two!

**Jeff:** *(Shocked)* What!...Who said that!

**Frog:** I did.

**Jeff:** *(Surprised)* I don't believe it!

**Milo:** You haven't heard anything yet. Reebit, I heard you had a good joke.

**Frog:** Yes, I do. Where was the first French fry made?

**Jeff:** Ahh...I don't know. Where?

**Frog:** Grease! Ha, ha...Where is the best place to eat a hamburger?

**Jeff:** I don't know. Where?

**Frog:** In your mouth!...How did Ronald McDonald celebrate his marriage to Wendy?

**Jeff:** How?

**Frog:** He gave her an onion ring!

**Businessman:** *(Jumps out of his chair and rushes over to Milo.)* This is amazing! I'll give you $20 for your frog.

**Milo:** No thanks.

**Businessman:** I'll make it $50.

**Milo:** I can't do it.

**Businessman:** I've got to have this frog. I'll give you $100!

**Milo:** $100 for my frog?

**Businessman:** Yes, will you sell it?

**Milo:** Hmmm…Okay.

**Businessman:** Fantastic! Here you are. *(Hands Milo the money and rushes out the door.)* I'm going to be rich, rich, rich…ha, ha…

**Waiter:** *(Starts to clear off Businessman's table. Takes the newspaper and folds it up.)*

**Jeff:** I can't believe you sold him that frog!

**Milo:** I can get another frog.

**Jeff:** How are you going to find another talking frog?

**Milo:** Talking frog?...That frog can't talk.

**Jeff:** But I heard him with my own ears.

**Milo:** That wasn't the frog, silly. It was the fly. The fly is a ventriloquist!

**Jeff:** *(Shocked)* A ventriloquist?

**Milo:** Yes. There isn't another fly like this one in the whole world.

**Jell:** This is fantastic! We'll make a million bucks!

**Waiter:** *(Spots the fly on the table and shouts.)* Don't move! *(Immediately he smashes the fly with the folded newspaper.)*

**Milo and Jeff:** *(Jump up from their chairs in wide-eyed horror.)*

**Waiter:** Don't worry! I got it. *(He looks at the end of the newspaper and flicks the dead fly off.)* Darn flies, I don't know where they all come from. *(Walks away.)*

**Milo and Jeff:** *(Mouths open and in shock they faint lifelessly to the ground.)*

The End

# The Balloon Contest

**Number of Participants:** Five or more

**Characters**: First Man, Second Man, three or more balloon blowers.

**Props:** Balloons

**Setting:** First Man and Second Man walk by a group of people who are blowing up balloons until they break.

## The Performance

**First Man:** What are they doing?

**Second Man:** Blowing up balloons.

**First Man:** Why?

**Second Man:** It's a contest.

**First Man:** Oh, what does the winner get?

**Second Man:** Nothing.

**First Man:** What does the loser get?

**Second Man:** He gets to buy more balloons. *(They walk off the stage.)*

The End

# The Burglar

**Number of Participants:** Two

**Characters**: Daddy and Burglar

**Costumes:** Burglar wears a mask

**Props:** Crib, doll, baby blanket, and handgun

**Setting:** The Daddy is pacing back and forth across the room carrying a crying child trying to put the baby to sleep. (The doll is wrapped in the blanket to look like a baby.) The baby soon falls to sleep.

## The Performance

**Daddy:** *(After getting the baby to sleep, he gently and quietly places him into a crib that is in the center of the stage.)* Phew!...I thought I'd never get him to go fall asleep.

**Burglar:** *(Sneaking into the room, he presses the gun into the Daddy's ribs.)* Stick 'em up!

**Daddy:** *(Placing the fingers to his lips)* Shhhhhh!

**Burglar:** *(Forcibly)* I said stick 'em up and no monkey business.

**Daddy:** Be quiet, you'll wake up the baby.

**Burglar:** This gun won't wake up anybody. It's got a silencer on it, and when I shoot you it won't make a sound.

13

**Daddy:** *(Becoming interested)* You say it won't make a sound?

**Burglar:** That's right. Nobody can hear a thing. It wouldn't wake up a soul.

**Daddy:** Not even the baby?

**Burglar:** No, not even the baby!

**Daddy:** *(Throwing up his hands)* Well, why didn't you say so. Go ahead and shoot!

The End

# The Bus Stop

**Number of Participants:** Four

**Characters**: Stooge, Bus Driver (Voice), First Man, Second Man

**Costumes:** Street clothes. Stooge wears clothing that easily identifies him from everyone else.

**Props:** A horn and a sign that reads "Bus Stop."

**Setting:** Stage is empty except for the sign. This skit is done in pantomime except for an offstage voice at the beginning. The offstage voice can be that of the Bus Driver or any other participant except the Stooge.

## The Performance

**Stooge:** *(Enters, walks to the Bus Stop sign, looks to the right in anticipation of the bus, and waits. As he is waiting he checks his pockets looking for a stick of gum. He pulls out a piece of gum, unwraps it, and begins chewing. He chews with exaggeration so audience can see his actions, occasionally looking at his watch and to the right for the bus.)*

**Voice:** *(Speaking loudly from offstage)* Hey you!

**Stooge:** *(Startled, looks around, and points to himself.)*

**Voice:** Yes, you! Are you taking the bus to town?

**Stooge:** *(Nods his head "yes" and continues chewing gum.)*

15

**Voice:** You know you can't get on the bus with that bubble gum.

**Stooge:** *(Stops chewing in mid motion and looks disappointed. Reluctantly he takes the piece of gum out of his mouth and looks around to see where to put it. No trash can in sight.)*

**Voice:** You better hurry the bus is coming. *(Bus honks its horn.)*

**Stooge:** *(He hears the beep of the horn and quickly looks side to side to find a place for the gum, spots the Bus Stop sign and sticks the gum on the post holding up the sign.)*

**Bus Driver:** *(Enters stage from the right shuffling along as if driving a bus and honks horn.)*

**Stooge:** *(Acts as if getting into the bus.)*

**Bus Driver:** *(Drives off the stage with Stooge following.)*

**First Man:** *(Enters and approaches bus stop, looks both ways looking for the bus, and begin to wait. His nose begins to tickle as a sneeze builds up. He lets loose with a big sneeze, which is contained by cupping his hands in front of his mouth. His hands are now wet. He looks at them and makes a disgusting face. He looks left and right for something to wipe them on. Finding nothing, he wipes his hands off on his pants. Continuing to wait for the bus, he leans over and places his hand on the post holding the bus stop sign. After a second or two he realizes that he put his hand on something. His hand is stuck to the post. He pulls and struggles briefly to free himself. The gum is stuck to his hand. He struggles to pull the gum off his hand. Eventually freeing the gum he throws it down on the street. He hears the bus driver honk his horn.)*

**Bus Driver:** *(Enters from right and honks his horn.)*

**First Man:** *(Acts as if getting into the bus.)*

**Bus Driver:** *(Drives off the stage with First Man.)*

**Second Man:** *(Enters and walks over to the bus stop. He looks right for the bus and continues to wait, slowly pacing back and forth. Suddenly, he stops as he steps on the gum. His foot is stuck to the pavement. He struggles to lift his foot. He struggles to free his foot then proceeds to pull the gum off the sole of his shoe. The Bus Driver honks his horn. Seeing the bus coming he sticks the gum to the sign post.)*

**Bus Driver:** *(Enters from the right and honks his horn.)*

**Second Man:** *(Acts as if getting into the bus.)*

**Bus Driver:** *(Drives off the stage with Second Man. After leaving the stage, he honks the horn and drives back to the bus stop from the left. This time Stooge is returning on the bus. The bus stops at the sign and lets Stooge off. Bus exits.)*

**Stooge:** *(Walks past the sign, stops, turns, looks at it, sees his gum, removes it from the post, puts in his mouth, and continues on his way.)*

The End

---

Note: The actors need to pay attention to where the imaginary gum is located. When setting up the stage before the show, place a piece of tape on the sign post and on the floor where the gum is supposed to be. The actors should make it look as if they are putting or removing the gum from the marked spots.

---

# Button Up

**Number of Participants:** Three

**Characters:** First Man, Second Man, Third Man

**Costumes:** Second Man and Third Man were vests. First Man does not.

**Props:** Stage money, sign that reads "Bus Stop."

**Setting:** The sign is in the center of the stage. First Man is standing by the sign. Second Man enters from the right side of the stage and walks to join him.

## The Performance

**First Man:** Good morning.

**Second Man:** Good morning. Waiting for the bus?

**First Man:** Yes. It ought to be by any minute. Say, that's a nice vest you're wearing.

**Second Man:** Why, thank you.

**First Man:** It has quite a number of buttons.

**Second Man:** I suppose so.

**First Man:** How long does it take you to button them all?

**Second Man:** I don't know.

**First Man:** I tell you what. I'll bet you a dollar you can't unbutton them all in 30 seconds.

**Second Man:** *(Smiling)* That's easy. You're on! *(Each man places a dollar on the floor.)*

**First Man:** *(Looking at his watch)* Ready, set, go!

**Second Man:** *(Easily unbuttons vest in allotted time.)* Ha, did it! *(He scoops up the money.)*

**First Man:** I bet you five dollars you can't BUTTON UP your vest in 30 seconds.

**Second Man:** Five dollars?...It's a deal. *(Both put five dollars on the ground.)*

**First Man:** *(Looking at watch)* Ready, set, go!

**Second Man:** *(Buttons vest starting from the top and working down.)* Finished! *(Thinking he's won, he bends over to pickup the cash. As he does so the First Man kicks him in the seat of the pants knocking him to the ground.)*

**First Man:** What do you think you're doing?

**Second Man:** I won the bet.

**First Man:** No you didn't. We had a bet on how fast you could button UP your vest. You buttoned it DOWN. *(He grabs the money.)* My bus is here I have to go. *(Walks off the stage leaving the Second Man still sitting on the floor.)*

**Third Man:** *(Enters and walks over to wait for the bus.)*

**Second Man:** *(Stands up and notices the vest Third Man is wearing and decides to pull the same trick on him. He looks at the audience and points to his vest and the other man's vest, winks, and nods mischievously.)* Nice vest.

**Third Man:** Thank you. *(He looks at vest proudly.)*

**Second Man:** *(Points candidly to the Third Man and smiles at the audience to let them know what he's thinking.)* It has quite a lot of buttons doesn't it?

**Third Man:** Yes, I guess so.

**Second Man:** *(He giggles to himself knowing he's gong to pull one over on this guy.)* I bet you a dollar you can't unbutton them all in 30 seconds.

**Third Man:** A dollar? Okay. It's a bet. *(Both men take out a dollar and place it on the ground.)*

**Second Man:** *(Looking at his watch)* Ready, set, go!

**Third Man:** *(He finishes unbuttoning in time.)* Finished!

**Second Man:** *(He giggles)* Well, it looks like you won. *(Giggles)* Say, that was too easy, I bet you can't BUTTON UP your vest in 30 seconds.

**Third Man:** I think I can.

**Second Man:** Want to bet?

**Third Man:** Sure. I bet you ten dollars I can do it in 30 seconds.

**Second Man:** *(Excited)* Ten dollars! Oh, boy. Yeah, I'll bet you ten dollars. *(Looks at audience)* This will be like stealing candy from a baby. Hee, hee. *(Both men put ten dollars on the ground.)* Are you ready?

**Third Man:** Yes, I'm ready.

**Second Man:** *(Snickers)* Okay. Ready, set, go!

**Third Man:** *(Buttons his vest from top to bottom.)*

**Second Man:** *(As Third Man is buttoning his vest, Second Man looks at the audience and giggles motioning that he is buttoning in the wrong direction.)*

**Third Man:** Finished! And under 30 seconds too. *(He quickly scoops up the money.)*

**Second Man:** *(Clinching his fist in victory.)* Yes! *(Thinking he trapped the man, giggles and looks at audience indicating that he had just pulled one over the this guy and continues to chuckle.)*

**Third Man:** Oh, my bus is here. *(Rushes off the stage.)* Good-bye.

**Second Man:** *(So wrapped up in his victory he doesn't pay close attention.)* Yeah, good-bye…What? Good-bye? *(Startled)* Hey!…Wait!…Come back…Stop. You didn't do it right…That's my money…Stop…Stop that bus! *(He runs off the stage in pursuit of the bus.)*

The End

# The Cat Lady

**Number of Participants:** Two

**Characters**: Thelma and Mildred

**Costumes:** Street clothes

**Props:** A box with holes in the lid.

**Setting:** Thelma is walking down the street when she meets Mildred.

## The Performance

**Thelma:** Hello, Midred.

**Mildred:** Hello, Thelma. *(Looking at the box)* What's in your box?

**Thelma:** A cat.

**Mildred:** A cat!

**Thelma:** Yes.

**Mildred:** What's the cat for?

**Thelma:** You see I've been dreaming about mice at night and I'm so sacred! So I got this cat to catch them.

**Mildred:** But the mice are only imaginary.

**Thelma:** I know. So is the cat. *(She exits)*

The End

# The Census Taker

**Number of Participants:** Two

**Characters**: Census Taker and Woman

**Costumes:** Street clothes. Woman wears an apron.

**Props:** Rolling pin.

**Setting:** The Census Taker knocks on Woman's door. Woman comes to the door holding a rolling pin and wearing the apron.

## The Performance

**Census Taker:** Hello, ma'am. *(Spotting the rolling pin in her hand)* I see you're making bread.

**Woman:** Yes, I was just about to roll out the dough. Can I help you?

**Census Taker:** I'm the county census taker and I'm here to get some information about you and your family for our records. May I ask you a few questions?

**Woman:** Okay. What do you want to know?

**Census Taker:** I understand you buried your grandfather last week?

**Woman:** Yes—I had to.

**Census Taker:** Why's that?

**Woman:** He was dead!

**Census Taker:** How about your grandmother? How is her health?

**Woman:** Oh, my grandmother is 87 and still doesn't need glasses.

**Census Taker:** Really?

**Woman:** Yeah...She drinks right out of the bottle.

**Census Taker:** What's your husband do for a living?

**Woman:** He's a realtor. We haven't had much success in the real estate market though. I think it's because we wants to sell our house complete—with the furniture and the kids.

**Census Taker:** Has he always wanted to be a realtor?

**Woman:** No. He's always wanted to be a stage magician and saw people in half.

**Census Taker:** Is he an only child?

**Woman:** Oh no, he's got several half-brothers and sisters.

**Census Taker:** How do you spend your income?

**Woman:** We spend 30 percent for shelter, 30 percent for clothing, 40 percent for food, and 20 percent for everything else.

**Census Taker:** But that adds up 120 percent.

**Woman:** I know and it seems to get worse every year!

**Census Taker:** Is your husband home now?

**Woman:** No. He's in jail.

**Census Taker:** Jail?

**Woman:** Yeah, he was put there for stealing a pig.

**Census Taker:** How could they prove he did it?

**Woman:** The pig squealed.

**Census Taker:** Do you have any children under the age of two?

**Woman:** Yeah, we have a new baby in our house.

**Census Taker:** I bet he reigns as king in you family now.

**Woman:** No—the Prince of Wails.

**Census Taker:** How is your health?

**Woman:** The doctor said I was way overweight.

**Census Taker:** What are you doing about it?

**Woman:** The doctor put me on a new diet with lots of fish oil and vegetable oil.

**Census Taker:** Does it work?

**Woman:** I don't know yet, I'm not thinner, but I don't squeak any more.

**Census Taker:** Any health problems in the family?

**Woman:** Last week my uncle swallowed a frog.

**Census Taker:** Goodness, did it make him sick?

**Woman:** Sick! He's liable to croak any minute!

**Census Taker:** I have just one more question. How old are you?

**Woman:** What? You can't ask a woman a question like that!

**Census Taker:** I need that information for my records.

**Woman:** That's too personal. I'm not going to tell you.

**Census Taker:** But everybody tells their age to the census taker.

**Woman:** Did the Hill sisters next door tell you their ages?

**Census Taker:** Why certainly.

**Woman:** Well, I'm the same age as they are.

**Census Taker:** Okay, I'll put it on record that you are as old as the Hills!

**Woman:** What! Why you... *(She lifts the rolling pin above her head as if to hit the Census Taker and chases him off stage.)*

The End

# The Check

**Number of Participants:** Three

**Characters**: Waitress, First Man, Second Man

**Costumes:** Waitress wears apron

**Props:** Two chairs and a table

**Setting:** Two men are eating dinner at a restaurant. They have just finished their meal and the waitress brings the check. She stands by the table waiting for them to pay.

## The Performance

**Waitress:** Here's your check.

**First Man:** Thank you. Hmmm. *(Picks up the check, looks at it, and gives it to Second Man.)* Here, you pay it.

**Second Man:** *(Looks at the check, hands it back to First Man.)* Ahh…No, you pay it.

**First Man:** *(Gives it back to Second Man.)* You pay it.

**Second Man:** No, I think you ought to pay for this one.

**First Man:** *(Hands it back to Second Man.)* But I paid for the last one.

**Both Men:** *(Look at the waitress)*

**Second Man:** *(To waitress)* Do you mind who pays this?

**Waitress:** No. I don't care who pays it, just so long as it gets paid.

**Second Man:** *(Hands her the check.)* Good. Here, then you pay it! *(Both men jump up and run off the stage with the waitress chasing after them.)*

The End

# The Chicken

**Number of Participants:** Three

**Characters**: Father (or Mother), Son, Doctor

**Costumes:** Street clothes

**Props:** None

**Setting:** The Father is speaking with the Doctor while his son is in the background acting like a chicken.

## The Performance

**Father:** What's wrong with my son Doctor?

**Doctor:** He has a very unusual condition. He thinks he is a chicken.

**Father:** A chicken?

**Doctor:** Yes, a chicken. That's why he cackles and struts around so. How long has he been acting like this?

**Father:** Oh, about ten years.

**Doctor:** *(Surprised)* Ten years! Why didn't you bring him in to see me before this?

**Father:** Because we needed the eggs.

The End

# The Classroom

**Number of Participants:** Five or more

**Characters**: Miss Hickymeyer, Peggy, Ronny, Claudia Wilkins, Joey

**Costumes:** Street clothes. Claudia's hair is in a mess.

**Props:** Teacher's desk or table and chairs for students.

**Setting:** Students are seated in a schoolroom ready to begin class. Joey enters the room crawling on his hands and knees.

## The Performance

**Teacher:** Good morning class.

**Students:** Good morning Miss Hickymeyer.

**Teacher:** *(Notices Joey crawling into class)* Joey, why are you crawling into class?

**Joey:** Because the class has already started and you said, "Don't anyone dare *walk* into my class late!"

**Teacher:** We start school precisely at nine o'clock.

**Joey:** That's okay. If I'm not here you can start without me.

**Teacher:** You're late almost every day. What is your excuse this time?

**Joey:** I overslept.

**Teacher:** You mean you sleep at home, too?...I thought you got plenty of sleep in class. I've had to punish you every day this week. What have you got to say?

**Joey:** I'm glad it's Friday!

**Teacher:** *(Annoyed)* Sit down. And try not to fall asleep.

**Joey:** Yes, Miss Hickymeyer.

**Teacher:** *(Notices Claudia's unkempt hair.)* Claudia, your hair's a disgrace. Have you combed it?

**Claudia:** No.

**Teacher:** What would you say if I came into class looking like that?

**Claudia:** I'd be too polite to mention it.

**Teacher:** Everybody get out a piece of paper and a pencil...Joey, where is your pencil?

**Joey:** I ain't got none.

**Teacher:** *(Shocked at his bad grammar.)* What?

**Joey**: I ain't got none.

**Teacher**: Joey, how many times have I told you not to say that? Now listen: I do not have a pencil, you do not have a pencil, they do not have a pencil. Now, do you understand?

**Joey:** Not really. What happened to all the pencils?

**Claudia:** *(Raises hand)* Miss. Hickeymeyer.

**Teacher:** Yes, Claudia.

**Claudia:** What are the biggest ants in the world?

**Teacher:** I'm not sure.

**Peggy:** *(Raises hand)* I know.

**Teacher:** Peggy, what are the biggest ants?

**Peggy:** Giants!

**Claudia:** *(Raises hand)* Miss Hickeymeyer.

**Teacher:** Yes, Claudia.

**Claudia:** Which pine has the longest needles?

**Peggy:** *(Raises hand)* I know.

**Teacher:** Peggy.

**Peggy:** A porcu-pine!

**Teacher:** Well, Peggy seems to have all the answers today. Since you're doing so well, name six animals that live in the Arctic?

**Peggy:** Ahh, a walrus, a seal, and…ahh…and four polar bears.

**Joey:** *(Begins to nod and fall asleep.)*

**Teacher:** Let's review some of our history lesson from yesterday. *(Sees Joey nodding off)* Joey, you're not falling asleep are you?

**Joey:** *(Startled)* Ahh...No. I heard every word.

**Teacher:** Joey, why were the Middle Ages also called the Dark Ages?

**Joey:** Ahh...well...I guess because there were lots of knights in those days.

**Teacher:** If you would have paid attention in class yesterday, and not fallen asleep, you would have known the answer. *(Looks at Peggy)* Peggy, who was Alexander Graham Bell Kowalski?

**Peggy:** He was the first telephone Pole.

**Joey:** I wish I went to school when you were a kid.

**Teacher:** Why is that, Joey?

**Joey:** Because there wouldn't have been so much history to learn.

**Teacher:** Let's work on our numbers. Joey, if you have four dollars in one pocket and twelve dollars in another, what have you got?

**Joey:** Someone else's pants on!

**Teacher:** Let me state it in another way. If you had four bananas, two oranges, and ten grapes, what would you have?

**Joey:** A fruit salad!

**Teacher:** Let's try it one more time. If I have four sandwiches and you have four sandwiches, what would we have?

**Joey:** Lunch!

**Teacher:** Ronny.

**Ronny:** Yes?

**Teacher:** Let's see if you can do any better. If you had six candy bars and I asked you for three, how many would you have left?

**Ronny:** Six!

**Teacher:** Let's say you gave one to Susan, one to Nancy, and one to Mary, what would you have then?

**Ronny:** Three new girl friends.

**Teacher:** Claudia, if you add 45 and 66, then divide the answer by 4, what would you get?

**Claudia:** The wrong answer.

**Teacher:** Maybe we will have better luck with English. Joey, give me a sentence using the words "defeat," "defense," and "detail."

**Joey:** Use all those words in one sentence?

**Teacher:** Yes.

**Joey:** Ahhh...Defeat of de dog went over defense before detail.

**Teacher:** *(Shakes head from sided to side and tries again)* Joey, I want you to correct this sentence: Girls is naturally more beautiful than boys.

**Joey:** *(Repeating the sentence)* Let's see, girls is naturally more beautiful than boys...Ahh...okay...Girls is artificially more beautiful than boys.

**Teacher:** Let me see if somebody else can do any better than you. Ronny.

**Ronny:** Yes, ma'am.

**Teacher:** Use "income" in a sentence.

**Ronny:** I opened the door and in come the cat.

**Teacher:** Wrong! Try "ransom."

**Ronny:** I saw a skunk and ran some distance away.

**Teacher:** No. Try "handsome."

**Ronny:** Hand some candy to me.

**Teacher:** *(Exasperated)* Your last chance is "gruesome."

**Ronny:** Since last year I grew some.

**Teacher:** Enough of this. Let's read the short essays you wrote for your homework last night. Claudia will stand up and read yours?

**Claudia:** Yes, ma'am. *(Reading)* The Tale of Two Taters by Claudia Wilkins. A Grade AAA Irish potato married a Grade AAA

Idaho potato. A fine grade potato, like Mr. Potato, would not marry anyone of any lesser class. Before long they had a little baby girl spudette—Grade AAA, of course. As she was growing up the guy spuds always had their eyes on her because she was a real sweet potato. But none of them could measure up to her standards. Then one day she announced to her father. "Dad, I want to marry the famous newsman Dan Rather." Her father was indignant. "Absolutely not, my dear. You can't marry him, he's just a commentator."

**Teacher:** Ah...thank you, Claudia.

**Claudia:** *(Sits down)*

**Teacher:** Peggy, will you read your essay?

**Peggy:** Yes. My essay is titled "My Grandpa Odd." My grandfather had a very unusual name. When he was born, his parents named him Odd, that's spelled O-d-d. In those days parents often named their children after important members of the family. Odd was named after my great-great-great-grandfather Duke Chesterfield Oddwellington. They just called him Odd for short. Besides, his parents didn't go to school and didn't know how to spell Oddwelllington. So he grew up as a little Odd. In school the kids used to make fun of his name and he hated it. He disliked his name all his life. He despised the name so much that when he died, he wouldn't allow the stonemason to put his name on his headstone. It was a blank tombstone containing only the dates of his birth and death. That's all it really needed. Now when people walk by, they look at it, kind of frown and say, "That's odd."

**Teacher:** Thank you Peggy. I would like... *(She is disrupted in mid-sentence)*

**Joey:** *(Has fallen asleep and begins to snore loudly.)* Snnooore!

**Teacher:** *(Angry)* JOEY! Wake up!

**Joey:** *(Startled and sleepy)* Ahh…yeah?

**Teacher:** If your father knew how badly you've behaved in class, he'd get gray hair overnight.

**Joey:** *(Smiles)* Really? He'd be please about that—he's bald!...*(School bell rings)*

**Teacher:** *(Exhausted)* Class dismissed.

**Students:** *(Dash out of class.)* Yeah!

The End

# David Copperbottom the Magician

**Number of Participants:** Two

**Characters**: Magician and Heckler

**Costumes:** Magician wears silly magic outfit or clown costume, Heckler wears street clothes.

**Props:** Sign with the words "The Amazing David Copperbottom." Plastic glass container filled with water, wooden block painted to look like a cupcake, fist-sized tooth made of white foam robber, chair, large pair of pliers, table (preferably a magician's table), foam rubber hammer.

**Setting:** Sign is displayed on the side of the stage. Magician is standing behind table, chair is behind him. A glass of water is on the table.

## The Performance

**Magician:** Welcome ladies and gentlemen, I the great magician, David Copperbottom will astound you tonight with extraordinary feats of magic. To start off, I will make this ordinary glass of water disappear before your very eyes. Yes, you heard me correctly, before your very eyes. I will not hide the glass under a cloth or behind a screen. I will perform this daring feat of magic before your very faces. Ready? Watch closely as I say the magic words…Hocus Pocahontas. *(Waves his hand above the glass. In one quick move he picks up glass and drinks the water.)* Ta-daa! The water has disappeared.

**Heckler:** *(Speaking from the audience)* Hey! You said you would make the "glass" of water disappear and only the water is gone what about the glass?

**Magician:** Oh. So you want the glass to disappear too? If you would please kindly look toward the door at the side of the auditorium. What do you see there? *(As everyone looks he quickly grabs the plastic glass and tosses it off the stage.)*

**Heckler:** I don't see anything.

**Magician:** That's right there isn't anything over there and there is nothing here either. The glass and water have disappeared...Since I'm doing so good with disappearances, I will now make this cupcake disappear.

**Heckler:** Hey! *(Comes up on stage.)* You're no magician. You're a phony. Anybody can do those things. You're nothing but a big fake.

**Magician:** Oh, yeah!

**Heckler:** Yeah! Look. I'll make that cupcake disappear too.

**Magician:** Oh, no! Don't, you might hurt yourself.

**Heckler:** Oh yeah, right. Like I'm going to hurt myself eating a cupcake like you got hurt making the water disappear.

**Magician:** Yes. My little nephew Milldew made them and he used cement instead of flour. It takes a miracle to eat one of these and you don't know magic and you may hurt yourself.

**Heckler:** Get out of here. Give me that cupcake. *(Grabs wooden block)*

**Magician:** *(Shocked)* No, don't!

**Heckler:** *(Bites into one and yells.)* Ohhhhhhh! *(Drops cake on the floor with a loud thud.)* My tooth! I broke my tooth!

**Magician:** Sit down and don't worry I'll fit it. *(Has Heckler sit in the chair then takes out a large pair of pliers and reaches toward him as if to pull Heckler's tooth.)*

**Heckler:** *(Leans back)* Oh, no you don't.

**Magician:** There's nothing to worry about. Remember, I'm a magician. You want your tooth fixed don't you?

**Heckler:** Well, okay.

**Magician:** *(Acts as though he is pulling a tooth from Heckler's mouth)*

**Heckler:** *(Squirms and makes muffled screams of pain.)* It's not working.

**Magician:** I know what's wrong. We forgot to say the magic word.

**Heckler:** What's the magic word?

**Magician:** Repeat the magic word after me...Cheese.

**Heckler:** Cheese? That's the magic word?

**Magician:** Just say it!

**Heckler:** *(Shrugs shoulders)* Okay, CHEESE!

**Magician:** *(During the conversation he has moved over to his table and pulled out a concealed foam rubber hammer. As soon as Heckler says "cheese" he hits him over the head with it. Heckler looks dazed. Magician quickly uses pliers to pull tooth before the Heckler regains his senses. He pulls out a large foam rubber tooth.)* I've got it!

**Heckler:** *(Mumbles, but can say no intelligible words. He motions to Magician and points to his mouth wanting to know what happened, why can't he talk?)*

**Magician:** What's that ? I can't hear you.

**Heckler:** *(Mumbles louder)*

**Magician:** I can't understand a word you're saying.

**Heckler:** *(Screams, but only loud mumbles come out.)*

**Magician:** Oh, you say you can't talk? *(He smiles)* My, my, isn't that just awful? *(He giggles)*…Hey, I've got another trick. I will now make a loudmouth disappear.

**Heckler:** *(Looks worried.)*

**Magician:** *(He grabs the pliers and moves toward the heckler.)*

**Heckler:** *(Mumbles a scream and runs off the stage.)*

**Magician:** *(Looks at the audience)* I love these disappearing acts, don't you?

The End

# Deadeye Dudley

**Number of Participants:** Two

**Characters**: Deadeye Dudley and Assistant

**Costumes:** Deadeye wears Cowboy clothing

**Props:** Cap gun, target, four balloons, scarf, a "BANG" gun, an apple, foam or rubber hammer, mirror, small table, two pins, sign which reads "Deadeye Dudley—World's Greatest Marksman."

**Setting:** Deadeye Dudley gives a sharpshooting demonstration. His Assistant is planted in the audience. On the stage is a table holding all the props.

## The Performance

**Deadeye:** *(Walks on stage carrying a target.)* Good evening, ladies and gentlemen. I am Deadeye Dudley, world's greatest sharpshooter. Tonight I am going to demonstrate my extraordinary skills of marksmanship, skills that have made me famous from here to Hoboken New Jersey, to London, Paris, and France. Yes, right before your very eyes you will see me do what seems like the impossible. But before I can continue any farther, I need a volunteer from the audience. Is there anyone who would like to volunteer? A volunteer please? Anyone? *(Spots man in front row)* You, sir.

**Assistant:** *(Surprised and points to himself)* Me?

**Deadeye:** Yes, you. Will come up here and assist me?

**Assistant:** *(Hesitant)* I...I...I...don't think I want to.

**Deadeye:** *(Insisting)* All these people came here to see a show. You wouldn't want to disappoint them would you?

**Assistant:** Well...I...I...I

**Deadeye:** What's the matter boy? You got something in your eye? *(Snickers)*

**Assistant:** *(Nervous)* I...I...don't know if it is safe.

**Deadeye:** *(Shocked)* Safe! Why of course you'll be safe. I NEVER miss! You have absolutely nothing to worry about. Now come on up here.

**Assistant:** *(Reluctantly goes up on stage)* Okay. But you promise I won't get hurt.

**Deadeye:** Trust me, you won't get hurt. I promise or my name isn't Nearsighted Jack.

**Assistant:** *(Shocked)* What!

**Deadeye:** *(Smiling)* Just kidding, now come over here. I want you to stand right here, do you understand?

**Assistant:** Yes.

**Deadeye:** Now hold this target up right here. *(He positions the bull's eye directly in front of Assistant's forehead.)* Okay?

**Assistant:** *(Holds target in front of his face with the bull's eye at forehead level.)* Okay.

**Deadeye:** *(Looks at audience and smiles.)*

**Assistant**: *(Realizing that if he holds the target in that position it could be dangerous, he quickly pulls it down.)* Say, wait a minute. I can't hold the target like that. It could be dangerous.

**Deadeye:** *(Snickering)* Yes, I know son. I was just kidding. Hold the target just above your head like this. *(He positions the target just over the Assistant's head.)*

**Assistant:** *(Questioning)* Like this? Isn't that a little too close to my head?

**Deadeye:** *(Reassuringly)* Why of course not. I'm Deadeye Dudley. I never miss. Now stand right there and don't move a muscle. Try to hold yourself as still as possible.

**Assistant:** *(Shaking)* Aaaaand, what are you going to do?

**Deadeye:** I'm going to put on this blindfold, then I'm going to walk ten paces, turn, and shoot a bull's eye, my boy. *(Using his scarf as a blindfold he puts it over his eyes.)*

**Assistant:** *(Scared)* Can I go home now?

**Deadeye:** *(Ignoring him)* Remember… *(He reaches out to grab Assistant by his shoulders, but can't find him. His hands move back and forth looking for the Assistant.)*

**Assistant:** I'm over here.

**Deadeye:** *(Locates his Assistant by blindly grabbing his face, to the displeasure of the Assistant, and finally positions his hands on each of the Assistant's shoulders as if to steady him.)* Remember… You must stand perfectly still. Any movement will… well, lets just say, don't move! You got it?

**Assistant:** Yes, don't move.

**Deadeye:** Good. *(He spins around trying to make a 180 degree turn so that he faces in the same direction as the Assistant, but ends up turning too much and ends up with his back towards the audience and facing the back of the stage.)*

**Assistant:** *(Worried)* Grabs him and points him forward in the right direction.

**Deadeye:** (Now facing in the same direction as the Assistant) Oh…thanks. Hold the sign up my boy.

**Assistant:** *(Lifting sign up over his head)* Okay.

**Deadeye:** Here we go. *(He holds cap gun close to his chest and begins to walk forward counting each step.)* One…two…three…

**Assistant:** *(Scared, he hunches down, with the target still held above his head, and follows directly behind Deadeye, step for step.)*

**Deadeye:** …nine…ten. *(He quickly spins around and fires off the gun. The blindfold is thin enough for him to see where the target is.)*

**Assistant:** *(He is standing directly behind Deadeye and hunched over at a level where Deadeye's gun points directly at the bull's eye. At the sound of the gun he lets out a high pitched yell and drops the target)* Yips!

**Deadeye:** *(Quickly pulls off the blindfold and picks up the target and smiles.)* See! A bull's eye! *(He pats the Assistant on the back)* Great job, my boy!

46

**Assistant:** Can I go back to my seat now?

**Deadeye:** Go back to your seat? We've just started. We haven't done the hard stuff yet!

**Assistant:** *(Looks sick)* The hard stuff?

**Deadeye:** Why yes, boy. The hard stuff. This was just a warm-up.

**Assistant:** *(Disappointed)* Ohhhhh...

**Deadeye:** *(He gives the Assistant two inflated balloons.)* Here. I want you to hold one of these in each hand with the right arm up and the left arm down.

**Assistant:** *(Holds right arm up high and left arm down to his side.)* Like this?

**Deadeye:** Yes, hold still. *(He backs up about 10 feet and pulls out his gun and aims.)*

**Assistant:** *(Scared, he begins to shake and balloons begin to shake.)*

**Deadeye:** *(Ordering)* Hold still!

**Assistant:** *(Closes his eyes and looks away, still shaking uncontrollably.)*

**Deadeye:** Don't move. Steady! *(Carefully aiming at the balloon above the Assistant's head)* One...two...three. *(He fires the gun.)*

**Assistant:** *(Taped onto one finger of each of the Assistant's hands is a pin. As soon as Deadeye says "three" and fires his* *gun, Assistant pokes the balloon in his left hand with the pin. With the sound of the gun, the Assistant jerks violently and shirks.)* Yikes!

**Deadeye:** *(Confused and looking surprised. He aimed at the upper balloon, but the lower one exploded.)* Why, ahhhh…ah…*(Smiles)* Right on!

**Assistant:** *(Concerned)* You hit the wrong balloon!

**Deadeye:** *(Bluffing)* Hogwash, my boy. That was my 90 degree shot. I shoot in one direction and the bullet goes in another. Hee..hee.

**Assistant:** I don't want to do this any more.

**Deadeye:** Have I hurt you, boy?

**Assistant:** Ahhh, no.

**Deadeye:** Then stop being such a sissy. Hold this balloon. *(Hands him another balloon.)* I want you to hold one balloon in each hand and position them right like this. *(He positions the balloons on either side of Assistant's head.)* Hold still. *(He backs up.)*

**Assistant:** Ba…ba…ba.

**Deadeye:** Ready? *(He aims)* One…two…three. *(He fires the gun.)*

**Assistant:** *(At the count of three he pops both balloons with the pins canceled in his hands. It appears as though one shot breaks both balloons.)* Why that's incredible! You shot both balloons with just one shot!

**Deadeye:** *(Proud)* That's what I keep telling you son. I'm Deadeye Dudley—world's greatest marksman!...Here hold this apple. *(He gives him an apple.)*

**Assistant:** *(Looks at the apple and begins eating it.)*

**Deadeye:** For my next trick I will... *(Sees Assistant eating the apple)* Hey! I said hold the apple, not eat it!...For my next trick I'm going to perform what I call the "William Tell Shot." What I want you to do is to place this apple on top of your head and I will shoot a hole right thought the middle.

**Assistant:** *(Starts to shake his head no.)* Noooo!

**Deadeye:** Son, don't you trust me?

**Assistant:** No.

**Deadeye:** Have I hurt you?

**Assistant:** Well, no.

**Deadeye:** Okay, then. Put the apple on your head.

**Assistant:** I...I...I...

**Deadeye:** There you go with the I's again?...I tell you what. You do this one last trick and I'll let you sit down. How's that sound?

**Assistant:** You mean if I help you with this one last trick, you will let me go?

**Deadeye:** Yes. That's what I mean. You help me with this trick and that's it. What do you say?

**Assistant:** Are you good at this trick?

**Deadeye:** Good? Why I've never missed…well, come to think of it I've never done this particular trick before, but that's besides the point. I promise you, you won't get hurt.

**Assistant:** *(Doubtful)* I don't know.

**Deadeye:** I tell you want. If I miss, you can take it out on me and beat me silly with this hammer. How's that?

**Assistant:** *(Seriously thinking)* Let me get this straight. If you don't shoot the center out of this apple, I can take this hammer and beat you silly? Is that right?

**Deadeye:** That's right. I never miss so I don't have anything to worry about.

**Assistant:** Okay. *(He balances the apple on his head. The bites he has taken out of the apple can help keep the apple in place.)*

**Deadeye:** *(Grabs the "BANG" gun and aims it carefully at the apple.)* Hold still. Ready? One…two…three. *(He fires the gun and a sign that says "BANG" jumps out.)*

**Assistant:** *(As the gun fires, his pants fall down.)* You missed! *(He is embarrassed and then angry. He quickly bends down grabs his pants in one hand, runs to the table, grabs the hammer with the other hand, and chases Deadeye off the stage.)*

The End

# Dental Floss

**Number of Participants:** Two

**Characters**: Dentist and Patient

**Costumes:** Dentist wears white coat.

**Props:** Chair or reclining chair, large Snickers candy bar

**Setting:** Patient is in dentist's chair.

## The Performance

**Dentist:** Open wide. Good grief! You've got the biggest cavity I've ever seen, the biggest I've ever seen.

**Patient:** All right, you don't have to repeat yourself!

**Dentist:** I didn't, that was an echo.

**Patient:** What are you going to do?

**Dentist:** I've got to fill it. What kind of filling do you want in your tooth?

**Patient:** How about Chocolate!

**Dentist:** Mmm... Will a Snickers bar do?

**Patient:** Yes.

**Dentist:** Here you go. (Hands him the candy bar)

**Patient:** Thanks. *(Gets up to leave.)*

**Dentist:** I'll see you again in 6 months. And don't forget to brush!

The End

# Dining Out

**Number of Participants:** Five

**Characters**: Customer, Waiter, Husband, Wife, Man

**Costumes:** Waiter wears an apron and has dish cloth over his arm. The rest are in street clothes.

**Props:** Three tables, four chairs, sign that reads "Restaurant", assorted food items.

**Setting:** The stage is set up like a restaurant. The Husband and Wife are sitting at one table and the Man at another. An empty table is between them. Customer walks in and is greeted by the Waiter.

## The Performance

**Customer:** Table for one please.

**Waiter:** Yes, sir. Right this way. Say, you look familiar. Have you been here before?

**Customer:** Why yes, I was here just a couple of weeks ago.

**Waiter:** Oh yes, I remember you now. You're the one who left a bus token as a tip.

**Customer:** Hey, bus tokens aren't cheap.

**Waiter:** Yeah, but you are. Here's you menu. Our special today is roast rack of lamb with mint sauce, and mushrooms and asparagus spears on the side, for only five dollars.

**Customer:** Only five dollars! Wow, that sounds great. I'll have the special.

**Waiter:** I'm sorry sir, but we're sold out of the special.

**Customer:** Then why did you even mention it? What else do you recommend?

**Waiter:** The porterhouse stakes are delicious. They come with a baked potato loaded with butter, bacon, sour cream, cheese, and diced green onions, served with fresh baked bread.

**Customer:** Mmmmm. That sounds delicious, I'll take it.

**Waiter:** I'm sorry sir, but we're all out of steaks.

**Customer:** What else do you recommend?

**Waiter:** Our roast chicken is very good.

**Customer:** Fine. I'll take the chicken.

**Waiter:** We're all out of chicken.

**Customer:** *(Disturbed)* Why do you keep recommending items you don't have?

**Waiter:** You keep asking me what's good, not what we have.

**Customer:** Okay then, what do you have?

**Waiter:** We have sheep's liver sautéed in goat's milk.

**Customer:** What else do you have?

**Waiter:** There's the braised cow's brains marinated in limburger cheese sauce topped with pickled herring.

**Customer:** No. Don't you have something ordinary like beef or fish?

**Waiter:** We have broiled codfish.

**Customer:** Fine. I'll take the broiled fish.

**Waiter:** Are you sure you wouldn't want the braised cow's brains. They're very good this time of year.

**Customer:** No. I don't like brains.

**Waiter:** Apparently. May I suggest the sheep's liver?

**Customer:** No. I don't like liver. Give me the fish.

**Waiter:** Okay. One broiled fish. Would you like anything else?

**Customer:** Yes, bring me a bowl of soup and a cup of coffee and make sure it's freshly ground.

**Waiter:** Very well, sir. *(He exits and returns with the coffee.)*

**Customer:** *(Tastes coffee)* Yuck! This coffee tastes like mud.

**Waiter:** Yes sir, as you requested that it be freshly *ground*…Here's your soup sir.

**Customer:** This looks good…wait a minute. There's a fly in my soup. Waiter, what's this fly doing in my soup?

**Waiter:** *(Looks at soup)* It looks like the backstroke.

**Customer:** I don't want the soup.

**Waiter:** May I bring you the fish sir?

**Customer:** Yes, I'm starved. So make it snappy.

**Wife:** *(Speaking to her husband)* Oh Henry, these cow's brains are absolutely delicious. I don't think I've tasted anything finer. I'm happy the waiter recommended them.

**Husband:** Yes, the sheep's liver is the best I've ever had; we must compliment the chef before we leave.

**Man:** *(He creates a ruckus by choking, spitting, gagging, and clinching his throat. He jumps up from the table with exaggerated motions of dying from eating something terribly nasty, than falls to the floor dead.)*

**Waiter:** *(He comes out with the fish, steps over the body on the floor, and stands by the customer.)*

**Customer:** What's wrong with him?

**Waiter:** Oh, he had the broiled fish....Don't worry, he does that all the time. Well, actually this is the first time he's eaten here. Oh well...Here's your fish sir.

**Customer:** Hey, you have you've got your thumb on my fish?

**Waiter:** I don't want it to fall on the floor again. It's a mess to clean up.

**Customer:** Could you bring me some mayonnaise please?

**Waiter:** I'm sorry, I can't.

**Customer:** Why not?

**Waiter:** It's dressing.

**Customer:** *(Takes a bite of his fish and makes a disgusting face)* Phew. This fish is terrible. I want the manager.

**Waiter:** I'm sorry sir, he isn't on the menu.

**Customer:** This fish is bad.

**Waiter:** *(Looks directly at the fish.)* You naughty fish, you!

**Customer:** I don't like this piece of cod. It doesn't taste as good as the one I ate here two weeks ago.

**Waiter:** I don't understand. It should taste exactly the same. It came from the same fish.

**Customer:** This food is giving me heartburn.

**Waiter:** Well, what did you expect—sunburn?

**Customer:** I have a complaint.

**Waiter:** A complaint? This is a restaurant, not a hospital.

**Customer:** I don't want the fish. I'll just have dessert. What do you recommend?

**Waiter:** Oh, the banana split is delicious.

**Customer:** Good, I've have a banana split.

**Waiter:** I'm sorry sir. We're all out of bananas.

**Customer:** Not this again! Do you have any ice cream?

**Waiter:** Yes sir—vanilla, chocolate, and strawberry.

**Customer:** I want a scoop of vanilla, a scoop of chocolate, a scoop of strawberry covered with hot fudge and whipped cream, and sprinkled with candy pieces and nuts.

**Waiter:** Would you like a cherry on top?

**Customer:** No thanks—I'm on a diet.

**Waiter:** I'll be right back. *(He leaves to get the dessert.)* Here you go sir.

**Customer:** *(Takes a spoonful, then closely examines the dessert pushing the cream from side to side only to discover it is only a bowl of cream.)* What's this? There's nothing here but whipped cream.

**Waiter:** Oh, I'm sorry sir. It fell on the floor and all that I could salvage was the cream.

**Customer:** I've had enough.

**Waiter:** Here's your bill sir. Will you be paying with cash or credit card?

**Customer:** Just put it on my account.

**Waiter:** What account?

**Customer:** On account that I don't have any money. *(He jumps up out of his chair and runs for the door.)*

**Waiter:** Ooooh you! *(Chases him out of the restaurant)*

The End

# The Doctor Knows Best

**Number of Participants:** Four

**Characters**: Doctor, Mrs. Peabody, Mr. Rosebotthem, Nurse

**Costumes:** Doctor wears white lab coat, nurse white nurse's uniform

**Props:** Two chairs, one for waiting room and one for the doctor's office, large syringe

**Setting:** Mr. Rosebotthem is sitting in the chair in the Doctor's waiting room. Mrs. Peabody enters and speaks with the Nurse.

## The Performance

**Mrs. Peabody:** I would like to see the Doctor.

**Nurse:** What's your problem?

**Mrs. Peabody:** I'm so big, I feel like a mountain! Is there anything you can do?

**Nurse:** Don't worry—we'll get you in peak condition.

**Mrs. Peabody:** That's not all. I keep stealing chairs. I can't seem to control myself.

**Nurse:** That's all right. Take a seat…The Doctor will be with you in a moment.

**Mrs. Peabody:** *(Examines chair Mr. Rosebotthem is sitting in, as if thinking about walking off with it.)*

**Nurse:** Mr. Rosebotthem, there's a mistake here on your information form.

**Mr. Rosebotthem:** *(Stands up and speaks with Nurse)* Where?

**Mrs. Peabody:** *(Sits in vacant chair)*

**Nurse:** *(Showing him her clipboard)* Right there...where it says, "In case of emergency, notify_____"

**Mr. Rosebotthem:** *(Looks at clipboard)* What's the problem?

**Nurse:** You said, "A doctor!"

**Mr. Rosebotthem:** Well, that's who I would notify in case of an accident.

**Doctor:** Nurse, send in the next patient.

**Nurse:** The Doctor is ready to see you now.

**Mr. Rosebotthem:** Thank you Nurse. *(Walks into the Doctor's office.)*

**Doctor:** What seems to be your trouble?

**Mr. Rosebotthem:** Doctor, I keep thinking I'm a goat. *(Jerks his head to the side and bellows like a goat.)* Baaaaaa.

**Doctor:** How long have you had this feeling?

**Mr. Rosebotthem:** Ever since I was a kid.

**Doctor:** *(Contemplating)* Mmmmm.

**Mr. Rosebotthem:** It's getting serious Doctor. I'm beginning to eat like a goat too. It's giving me indigestion. This morning I swallowed a roll of film.

**Doctor:** Don't worry. Nothing serious will develop…Do you have any other symptoms?

**Mr. Rosebotthem:** I hear ringing in ears. What should I do?

**Doctor:** Answer it.

**Mr. Rosebotthem:** What do you think is my problem?

**Doctor:** I believe you have a duel personality—goat and human personalities coexisting together as one entity all together signally as one joined jointly as one…I can treat only one of you, the other will have to see a veterinarian.

**Mr. Rosebotthem:** Is there anything you can do for me right now?

**Doctor:** Yes, I'll have the Nurse give you a shot. That always helps in cases like this. *(Calling for the Nurse)* Nurse!

**Nurse:** Yes, Doctor.

**Doctor:** Give this man a shot and tell the next patent to come in.

**Nurse:** Mrs. Peabody is next. But there are several others here to see you.

**Doctor:** How many?

**Nurse:** Seven of them claim a giant blood-sucking mosquito attacked them!

**Doctor:** Yes, I know. There's a nasty bug going around…Give them each a shot, that should help.

**Nurse:** There's another patient who just came in who is very frantic and demands to see you immediately. He says it's an emergency.

**Doctor:** What's his problem?

**Nurse:** He says he is shrinking. He's twelve inches shorter today than he was yesterday.

**Doctor:** Tell him to calm down. He's just going to have to be a little patient.

**Nurse:** There's also a man here who claims he's invisible.

**Doctor:** Well, you'll just have to tell him I can't see him right now…

**Nurse:** Yes, Doctor. I'll send in Mrs. Peabody… *(Speaking to Mrs. Peabody.)* the Doctor will see you now.

**Doctor:** Good morning, Mrs. Peabody, I haven't seen you for a long time.

**Mrs. Peabody:** I know, Doctor, I've been sick.

**Doctor:** Well, what can I do for you today?

**Mrs. Peabody:** Doctor, I'm so tired, I feel like an old broken down bus.

**Doctor:** Well, park yourself over here. *(Motions to chair)*

**Mr. Peabody:** Doctor, I can't sleep at night. I keep having the same dream about a door with a sign. I push and push but I can never push it open.

**Doctor:** What does the sign say?

**Mrs. Peabody:** "Pull."

**Doctor:** Mrs. Peabody, do you have any other complaints?

**Mrs. Peabody:** I've got a pain in my lower back. *(She places her hand on her lower backside.)*

**Doctor:** Yes, I see, we'll have to get to the bottom of this.

**Mrs. Peabody:** I also feel like I'm on pins and needles.

**Doctor:** Hummm, I see your point…Anything else?

**Mrs. Peabody:** I feel strange at times. I think I can see into the future.

**Doctor:** On really? When did this start?

**Mrs. Peabody:** Next Tuesday.

**Doctor:** Hmmm.

**Mrs. Peabody:** That's not all, sometimes I think I'm becoming invisible.

**Doctor:** Yes, I beginning to see that you're not all there. *(Doctor begins his examination)* Open your mouth and say ahh.

**Mrs. Peabody:** Ahhhhhhhhhhhhhh.

**Doctor:** Hmmmm.

**Mrs. Peabody:** What's wrong Doctor?

**Doctor:** Well, Mrs. Peabody, I have some good new for you, and some bad news. Which would you like to hear first?"

**Mrs. Peabody:** The bad news, please.

**Doctor:** Well, the bad news is that we'll have to amputate both your feet.

**Mrs. Peabody:** And the good news?

**Doctor:** We just had a cancellation and can squeeze you in tomorrow at 2 o'clock.

**Mrs. Peabody:** Wait. I don't want my feet amputated. Isn't there anything else you can do for me?

**Doctor:** Well yes, there is one more thing we can do.

**Mrs. Peabody:** Really, what?

**Doctor:** We can give you a shot. I love shots. Shots are good for practically everything from foot fungus to bad breath. There's almost nothing a little shot won't fix. And it will only cost you $50.

**Mrs. Peabody:** *(Frightened)* What! NO, NO, NOOOO! I don't like getting shots. They hurt.

**Doctor:** This won't heart a bit. Trust me. *(He grabs large syringe and steps toward Mrs. Peabody.)*

**Mrs. Peabody:** *(Starts screaming hysterically)* Yeaow, ouch, owoooooooo! Stop, stop, stop, you're killing me! Owoooooooo!

**Doctor:** *(Holding syringe)* Stop screaming. I haven't even touched you yet.

**Mrs. Peabody:** *(Speaking as if in great pain)* I know, but you're standing on my foot.

**Doctor:** Oh, sorry. Are you ready?

**Mrs. Peabody:** *(Closes eyes tightly and braces for shot)* Okay.

**Doctor:** This won't hurt a bit. *(Puts cotton swab on arm to prepare for shot.)*

**Mrs. Peabody:** Owwwwww!

**Doctor:** What are you yelling for? I haven't given you the shot yet, that was just the cotton swab.

**Mrs. Peabody:** It hurt.

**Doctor:** Hold this piece of cotton against your arm right here. *(While Mrs. Peabody is looking at arm, the doctor quickly injects the needle into the other arm.)*

**Mrs. Peabody:** *(Surprised)* Ouch!...Hey, what did you do?

**Doctor:** I gave you your shot. Now that wasn't so bad was it?

**Mrs. Peabody:** No, I guess not.

**Nurse:** *(Enters and whispers in Doctor's ear than leaves.)*

**Doctor:** You're ready to go, but I'll have to charge you $200 for the shot.

**Mrs. Peabody:** But you said it would be only $50.

**Doctor:** Yes, but you yelled so much you scared off three other patients.

**Mrs. Peabody:** One more question Doctor.

**Doctor:** Yes, what is it?

**Mrs. Peabody:** It's about my baby. He's always crying. Why does he cry so much?

**Doctor:** Well, if you had no hair and no teeth and your legs were so weak you couldn't stand up, you'd be crying too!

**Mrs. Peabody:** Thank you Doctor. I feel so much better every time I see you.

The End

# The Dog Act

**Number of Participants:** Two

**Characters**: Animal Trainer and Assistant

**Costumes:** Street clothes

**Props:** Hula hoop and stuffed dog

**Setting:** Animal Trainer enters stage carrying his trained dog.

## The Performance

**Trainer:** Good evening ladies and gentlemen, boys and girls, Moms and Dad, brothers and sisters, aunts and uncles, and everyone else here tonight. Have I missed anybody? *(Looks around the audience.)* I am Professor Xerox—animal trainer! And this is my trained dog, Snert. Say "Hi" to the audience Snert. *(Trainer shakes the dog and barks "Ruff, ruff.")* That a boy, Snert! Snert is a highly trained animal. Watch this. (He sets the dog on the ground) Sit, boy, sit! *(Dog sits there motionless)* See! He obeys. (Shouting out another command) Stay, stay boy, stay! *(Dog sits motionless. Trainer looks at the audience)* Didn't I you. He obeys my every command. *(Giving another command)* Snert, roll over, roll over. *(Trainer standing close to the dog tips him over with a nudge from his foot.)* That a boy! Now we are ready for the hard stuff. I need my assistant…will you come out here please.

**Assistant:** Enters stage carrying hula hoop.

**Trainer:** *(Stands the dog back up)* Snert will now jump through this hoop.

68

**Assistant:** *(Holds the hoop up, standing about eight feet in front of the dog.)*

**Trainer:** *(Standing to the side of the dog.)* Okay, Snert, when you are ready jump, through the hoop. *(Nothing happens)* Jump through the hoop, Snert. *(He makes motions with his arms for the dog to jump.)* Go ahead jump Snert, jump! Jump through the hoop! *(Nothing happens and Trainer is getting upset.)* Jump through the hoop Snert. *(Looks at the audience.)* This is a dangerous trick and sometimes Snert needs to build up courage. *(Looks back at the dog and speaks in a stern voice)* Jump through the hoop Snert! Jump! *(Walks up behind the dog and points to the hoop)* Jump! Jump! *(He quickly kicks the dog propelling it up and through the hoop. The Trainer smiles.)* That a boy, Snert! *(Trainer bows to the audience and he and the Assistant exit.)*

The End

# The Dog License

**Number of Participants:** Two plus a dog (or a person playing a dog)

**Characters**: Boy, Policeman, Dog

**Costumes:** Policeman wears uniform

**Props:** None

**Setting:** Boy is walking his dog down the street when they meet a policeman.

## The Performance

**Policeman:** Say, sonny.

**Boy:** Yes, officer?

**Policeman:** *(Looks at dog)* Has your dog got a license?

**Boy:** Oh, no. He's not old enough to drive. *(Walks off stage)*

The End

# The Eye Test

**Number of Participants:** Two

**Characters**: Doctor (Optometrist) and Patient

**Costumes:** White coat for doctor.

**Props:** Easel with four eye charts containing rows of random letters of different sizes, chair, and a set of large eyeglasses.

**Setting:** Patient enters Doctor's office.

## The Performance

**Doctor:** Come in and have a seat.

**Patient:** Thank you.

**Doctor:** Now what seems to be your problem?

**Patient:** *(Wearing a pair of very large eyeglasses.)* I think I need new glasses.

**Doctor:** Okay. Let me check your eyes. *(He points to the eye chart which is filled with small letters.)* Can you read this?

**Patient:** *(Straining)* No.

**Doctor:** *(He puts up another chart with bigger mixed letters.)* Can you read this?

**Patient:** No.

**Doctor:** *(He puts up another chart with bigger letters.)* How about this?

**Patient:** Can't read a thing.

**Doctor:** *(Takes out chart with one big backwards letter "E")* Surly you can read this one?

**Patient:** *(Looking carefully and shakes his head)* No.

**Doctor:** *(Surprised)* What! You mean you can't even see this letter?

**Patient:** Oh, I can see the letters fine, I just can't pronounce the words.

The End

# Fire! Fire!

**Number of Participants:** Three or more

**Characters**: Tramp, Cleaning Lady or Janitor, Fireman (may be one or more firemen)

**Costumes:** Tramp wears old worn out clothing, Fireman wears a fire hat.

**Props:** Old gunnysack, candle stick and holder, frying pan, rubber chicken, two buckets of water, bucket of popcorn, broom, large colorful handkerchief, horn, kazoo, old boot, brightly colored spotted or stripped boxer shorts, and a box of matches.

**Setting:** Tramp carrying the gunnysack over his shoulder enters the empty stage. This performance is done mostly in pantomime.

## The Performance

**Tramp:** *(Enters whistling merrily to himself as he wanders around the stage looking for a spot to sit down. Finds a spot and sits down. He opens his gunnysack and pulls out a kazoo and plays a few notes and puts it aside, pulls out an old boot and puts it aside. Looks deep and pulls out a pair of boxer shorts, opens them up so audience can get a look at them, quickly bunches them together and looks embarrassed then adds them to the pile. A fry pan is pulled out and added to the pile. He pulls out a candle on a candle stick, smiles, and carefully places it in front of him. He pulls out a box of matches and lights the candle. He grabs the fry pan, smiles, licks his lips, and rubs his stomach as if hungry. He pulls out of the sack a handkerchief, opens it up, and blows his nose in it. Offstage* *someone honks the horn into the microphone as he blows his nose. He wipes his nose, opens up the hanky and tucks one edge into this shirt collar to cover his shirt while he eats. He then rummages around in his gunny sack and pulls out a rubber chicken. The chicken is placed in the fry pan and the pan is held over the candle. He rubs his stomach and smacks his lips in anticipation of the meal.)*

**Cleaning Lady:** *(Wanders onto the stage sweeping the floor. She looks up, turns her head from side to side sniffing. She continues sniffing trying to locate where the smoke is coming from. Slowly she walks toward the Tramp. Spotting the fire, in alarm he shouts.)* Fire! Fire!, Fire! Fire!

**Fireman:** *(Rushes onto the stage carrying a bucket full of water.)*

**Cleaning Lady:** *(Points in the direction of the Tramp.)* Fire!

**Fireman:** *(Throws the water on the Tramp and exits.)*

**Cleaning Lady:** *(Relieved, exits)*

**Tramp:** *(Looks bewildered. He picks up his stuff, puts them under his arm and looks for another spot to have lunch. He sits down and begins cooking his chicken again.)*

**Cleaning Lady:** *(Enters the stage sweeping. She stops, sniffs the air, looks around and spots the fire and yells.)* Fire! Fire!, Fire! Fire!

**Fireman:** *(Rushes in and douses Tramp with another bucket of water, then exits.)*

**Cleaning Lady:** *(Exits)*

**Tramp:** *(Upset, grabs his stuff and begins looking for another dry spot. He wanders into the audience and sits down right in front of someone and begins the routine again.)*

**Cleaning Lady:** *(Enters, smells smoke, looks for it, spots the fire and yells.)* Fire! Fire!, Fire! Fire! *(Points to the Tramp)*

**Fireman:** *(Races out, heads toward the Tramp, and throws the contents of the bucket at the Tramp and the audience. However, this time the bucket is filled with popcorn instead of water. Audience is fooled in believing they are getting doused with water.)*

**Tramp:** *(Points to audience, laughs, and runs off.)*

The End

# The Flea Circus

**Number of Participants:** Four or more

**Characters**: First Man, Second Man, a group of two or more people

**Costumes:** Street clothes

**Props:** A sign reading "Flea Circus."

**Setting:** The sign is on the stage. First Man and Second Man walk by a group of people who are crawling around on the ground as if looking for something.

## The Performance

**First Man:** What are they doing?

**Second Man:** Looking for the trained flea.

**First Man:** I bet he's hard to find.

**Second Man:** Yeah, his owner thinks he might have run off.

**First Man:** Oh, what with another flea?

**Second Man:** No, with a dog.

The End

# The Gambler

**Number of Participants:** Two

**Characters**: Father and Principal

**Costumes:** Principal wears a beard

**Props:** None

**Setting:** Father is visiting with son's Principal.

## The Performance

**Principal:** Hello, Mr. Smithers.

**Father:** Hello, Principal.

**Principal:** Mr. Smithers, I have some good news! I think I've cured your son of gambling.

**Father:** Really! I've tried for years. How did you accomplish it?

**Principal:** I used elementary psychology. This morning he looked at my beard and asked me if it was real. I said it was. He said it looked fake and bet me ten dollars that it was false. So I took him up on the bet.

**Father:** What happened?

**Principal:** Of course, my beard is real. So, I let him pull on my beard. I won the bet and he lost ten dollars. I'm sure that will cure him of gambling!

**Father:** *(Distraught)* Oh, no!

**Principal:** *(Surprised)* What's the matter?

**Father:** Last night he bet me twenty-five dollars that you'd let him pull your beard!

**Principal and Father:** *(Feeling stupid)* Ohhhhh!

The End

# Get-To-Know-You

**Number of Participants:** Two

**Characters**: First Man and Second Man

**Costumes:** Street clothes

**Props:** None

**Setting:** First Man knocks on Second Man's front door.

## The Performance

**First Man:** Hi

**Second Man:** Can I help you?

**First Man:** We just moved in next door and we'd like to have a get-to-know-your-neighbors party.

**Second Man:** That sounds good.

**First Man:** Nothing too fancy. Maybe barbecue a few steaks, have a little wine, some music, and of course cake and ice cream for dessert.

**Second Man:** That sounds great.

**First Man:** Just my wife and two kids, and four or five of our friends.

**Second Man:** Okay.

**First Man:** How about next Saturday?

**Second Man:** We're not doing anything that day. Sure, that sounds great.

**First Man:** Wonderful. What time would you like us to be here?

**Second Man**: What?

**First Man:** Yeah, what time should I tell everyone to show up?

**Second Man:** Get out of here. *(Chases First Man away)*

The End

# Good Friends

**Number of Participants:** Two

**Characters**: Bobby and Dexter

**Costumes:** Street clothes

**Props:** Telephone, table, hat, and coat

**Setting:** Bobby is walking across the living room as telephone rings.

## The Performance

**Bobby:** *(Picks up phone)* Hello.

**Dexter:** Hey Bobby, is that you?

**Bobby:** Yes. Who is this?

**Dexter:** It's me, Dexter.

**Bobby:** *(Cheerfully)* Oh, hi buddy boy. How's it going?

**Dexter:** Fine. What's going on with you?

**Bobby:** Why nothing is going on. I was getting ready for bed.

**Dexter:** Well, then why did you call me?

**Bobby:** I didn't call you. You called me!

**Dexter:** I did?...Oh yeah. I did...What did you want?

**Bobby:** I didn't want anything. You called me Remember?

**Dexter:** Oh, right. Ahhh…we're good friends aren't we Bobby?

**Bobby:** Sure we are, good buddy. Is there something I can do for you? You know all you have to do is ask. That's what friends are for, right?

**Dexter:** Right. I was calling to ask if you would do me a big favor.

**Bobby:** Sure, you're my pal, anything you want it's yours. Just ask.

**Dexter:** Thanks. I knew you wouldn't let me down. Listen, I need to borrow $100…

**Bobby:** *(Raising voice)* Hello!…What?…I can't hear you. There must be something wrong with the connection.

**Dexter:** *(Speaking louder)* I said, I need to borrow $100…

**Bobby:** What was that? Speak louder.

**Dexter:** I need $100…

**Bobby:** This phone just isn't working right. I can't hear a word you're saying. I'll talk to you later. Bye. *(Hangs up phone)* Phew…I got out of that one.

**Dexter:** *(Immediately calls back)*

**Bobby:** *(Phone rings.)* Oh-oh, that must be Dexter. *(Speaking to the phone as if the caller can hear him)* I'm not home! *(Quickly grabs his hat and coat and dashes out the door.)*

The End

# The Graduate

**Number of Participants:** Three

**Characters**: College Graduate, Ervin, Patrick

**Costumes:** Mortarboard hat for graduate

**Props:** Diploma which reads "Deeploma, Institute of Edgeecation"

**Setting:** Ervin is on stage. Graduate enters wearing mortarboard hat and holding diploma rolled up and tied with red ribbon.

## The Performance

**Graduate:** *(Excited)* Hey Ervin, I just gladgeeated from college!

**Ervin:** You mean "graduated."

**Graduate:** Yah, I just gladgeeated. See my diploma.

**Ervin:** Let's see. *(Opens diploma looks at it and shows audience)* It says "Deeploma, awarded by the Institute of Edgeecation."

**Graduate:** Yah, I just gladgeeated. That means I am edgeecated. *(Smiles and looks dumb)*

**Ervin:** So you're smart aye?

**Graduate:** Yep. I'm a college gladgeeate.

**Ervin:** Ok, if you're so smart you won't mind if I ask you a few questions to test your knowledge.

**Graduate:** Nope, go right ahead, Ervin.

**Ervin:** What do you call the small rivers that run into the Nile?

**Graduate:** Oh, that's easy. They're juveniles.

**Ervin:** Ok, which direction does the Mississippi River run?

**Graduate:** Downhill, silly.

**Erwin:** Here's a math question.

**Graduate:** Oh, good. I like numbers.

**Erwin:** If you mowed the lawn for twenty-five people and they each paid you ten dollars, what would you get?

**Graduate:** That's easy. I'd get a new bicycle. The one I have now has a flat.

**Erwin:** Let's try some history. What did Paul Revere say after his famous ride?

**Graduate:** Whoa!

**Ervin:** Let's try one more. Where was the Declaration of Independence signed?

**Graduate:** What kind of decoration?

**Ervin:** Not decoration. Declaration of Independence. The document that our country's founding fathers signed during the Revolutionary War.

**Graduate:** Oh, that declaration. It was signed at the bottom of the paper…Ervin you tried to trick me, but it didn't work.

**Ervin:** You're unbelievable!

**Graduate:** Any more questions Ervin?

**Ervin:** Yes. If you're a gladgeeate and are so smart, see if you can answer this riddle.

**Graduate:** A riddle?

**Ervin:** Yeah, it's kind of like a test.

**Graduate:** Oh, I'm good at that.

**Ervin:** Who is this?…It's not my sister and it's not my brother, but it's the child of my father and mother.

**Graduate:** Let's see. It's not my sister and it's not my brother, but it's the child of my father and mother. *(Looks puzzled)* Hmmmm. *(Mumbles as if repeating the riddle to himself.)*

**Ervin:** Come on, who is it? Think. It's not my sister and it's not my brother, but it's the child of my father and mother.

**Graduate:** Hmmm. Got it! That was easy.

**Ervin:** Ok, who is it?

**Graduate:** It's the President of the United States!

**Ervin:** What? Noooo! It's somebody you know. Try again.

**Graduate:** Ok, somebody I know. Ahhh…Oh, I know who it is! It's Aunt Clydesdale.

**Ervin:** No. Think again. The person is right here in this room. *(He looks at Graduate from top to bottom as if giving him a hint.)* It's not my sister and it's not my brother, but it's the child of my father and mother. Who is it?

**Graduate:** Hmmmm. (Smiles and points into audience) The guy in the first row?

**Ervin:** No! Do you have any idea who it is?

**Graduate:** *(Mumbles part of the riddle)* It's not my sister or brother, but a child of…

**Ervin:** All right. I'll give you the answer. It's not my sister or brother. So it has to be ME! I'm the child of my father and mother.

**Graduate:** Oh yeah. Dugh. *(Snickers and smiles as if the answer was obvious.)*

**Ervin:** I would think a graduate from the prestigious "Institution of Edgeecation" would be able to figure out a simple riddle like that.

**Graduate:** Well, Ervin it's daytime now and I went to night school…Ask me the riddle again later tonight.

**Ervin:** I don't need to ask you again, you already know the answer now.

**Graduate:** Oh, yeah. I forgot. Hey, Ervin here comes Patrick. Let me try the riddle on him. He's not a gladgeeate like me, so it may take him a little longer to get the right answer…Hi Patrick.

**Patrick:** Hi guys.

**Graduate:** Patrick, I've got a riddle for you. See if you can figure it out.

**Patrick:** Okay.

**Graduate:** Who is this?… It's not my sister and it's not my brother, but it's the child of my father and mother.

**Patrick:** Let's see. *(He thinks and mumbles to himself.)* Why, it's you!

**Graduate:** Wrong, hee, hee. You're so dumb. It's ERVIN!

The End

# A Hard Hitting Act

**Number of Participants:** Five or more

**Characters**: Stooge, First Man, Second Man, two or more companions

**Costumes:** Normal clothes or clown costumes

**Props:** Rolled up newspapers

**Setting:** The Stooge is being hit over the head with newspapers by his two companions. Two others (First Man and Second Man) observe.

## The Performance

**First Man:** Gracious, what are they doing?

**Second Man:** Trying to knock some sense into him.

**First Man:** Doesn't it hurt?

**Second Man:** Sure!

**First Man:** Doesn't he mind?

**Second Man:** No.

**First Man:** How come?

**Second Man:** It feels so good when they stop.

The End

# Help Wanted

**Number of Participants:** Two

**Characters**: Mr. Harpsichord and Sev

**Costumes:** Street clothes

**Props:** Kazoogle (a kazoo inserted in the end of a bugle or other wind instrument in place of the ordinary mouthpiece), a small step ladder, a "Help Wanted" sign, and a sign which reads "Harpsichord Music."

**Setting:** Signs are displayed in the center of the stage. Mr. Harpsichord enters from one end and Sev from the other. Sev is carrying the kazoogle and ladder.

## The Performance

**Sev:** Are you Mr. Harpsichord?

**Harpsichord:** Yes.

**Sev:** I'm here in response to your help wanted ad.

**Harpsichord:** You want a job?

**Sev:** Yes.

**Harpsichord:** Do you know anything about music?

**Sev:** Yes. I love music. I would make a great salesclerk for your music store.

**Harpsichord:** What's your name?

**Sev:** Seven and three eights.

**Harpsichord:** What?

**Sev:** Seven and three eights.

**Harpsichord:** How did you ever get a name like that?

**Sev:** Well, when I was born my parents didn't know what to name me. So they picked a name out of a hat...You can call be Sev.

**Harpsichord:** Do you have any experience?

**Sev:** I have lots of experience.

**Harpsichord:** What was your last job?

**Sev:** I used to be a pediatrician.

**Harpsichord:** *(Surprised)* What happened?

**Sev:** I realized that I had little patients...So I quit.

**Harpsichord:** What did you do before that?

**Sev:** Well, my first job was as a professional bungee jumper. But they let me go.

**Harpsichord:** What then?

**Sev:** Then I worked in a bean factory, but I got canned...After that I worked in a blanket factory, but it folded...Then I worked in a woman's clothing store, but they gave me the pink slip…So now I'm here looking for a job with you.

**Harpsichord:** My life is music. I love classical music the most— Bach, Beethoven, Brahms. Our whole family is involved with music. My twelve year old son has been playing the piano for *eight* years.

**Sev:** Really, aren't his fingers tired?

**Harpsichord:** My father is a gifted musician. He plays the piano by ear.

**Sev:** Oh, that's nothing. My father fiddles with his whiskers.

**Harpsichord:** We require all employees to be punctual. Work starts at precisely 8:00 am every morning.

**Sev:** I'm very punctual. I always follow the same routine. I get up at 7:00 am every morning no matter what time it is.

**Harpsichord:** You need to know music to work here. Can you play any musical instruments?

**Sev:** Yes, I brought my instrument with me. *(He shows him his kazoogle.)*

**Harpsichord:** What is that?

**Sev:** It's a kazoogle.

**Harpsichord:** A kazoogle?

**Sev:** Yes, a kazoogle.

**Harpsichord:** *(Pointing to his step ladder)* What's the ladder for?

**Sev:** Oh, I use that so I can reach the high notes.

**Harpsichord:** Let's hear you play.

**Sev:** Okay. *(He begins playing a simple, but lively tune.)*

**Harpsichord:** (Irritated, holds hands to his ears) Enough!...Can you play anything else?

**Sev:** Hum a few bars and maybe I can fake it.

**Harpsichord:** No, can you play something different?

**Sev:** Here's a different song. *(He begins playing another lively song.)*

**Harpsichord:** No, no, no! Can you play any other instrument?

**Sev:** You mean like the piano or clarinet?

**Harpsichord:** Yes.

**Sev:** No. I just play the kazoogle. The thing about the kazoogle is that the more you hear it, the better you like it. Watch. *(He begins playing another tune.)*

**Harpsichord:** No. Stop! Stop!...I can't stand it! *(Covers his ears. Trying to block out the sound of the kazoogle he begins making a loud noise.)* Ahhhhhhhhhh!

**Sev:** *(Continues to play)*

**Harpsichord:** *(Jumps up, runs wildly around in a circle trying to get away from the irritating music and then runs off the stage.)* Ahhhhhhhhh!

**Sev:** *(Continuing to play, he follows closely behind Harpsichord as he runs around and off the stage.)*

The End

# The Hot Dog Stand

**Number of Participants:** Two

**Characters**: Vender and Customer

**Costumes:** Street clothes, vender wears an apron.

**Props:** Hot dog and bun, small cart on wheels with words "Hot Dogs" written on it.

**Setting:** Customer enters empty stage apparently looking for something.

## The Performance

**Customer:** Where is he? He used to be right here, but I don't see him. *(Looks at audience)* Hey, have you seen the hot dog vender? I've been looking everywhere and I can't find him.

**Vender:** *(Enters pushing hot dog stand.)* Hot dogs! Get a big juicy hot dog right here. Hot dogs! Hot dogs!

**Customer:** Well there you are. I've been looking all over for you.

**Vender:** You look familiar. Have I served you before?

**Customer:** Yes, about a year ago.

**Vender:** Oh, yes that's right now I remember.

**Customer:** *(To audience)* That's what I like about this guy. No matter how often you may come, he always remembers you and knows exactly how you like your hot dog, even if you've only been here one time, and come back a year later. He still remembers exactly how you like it. He never forgets.

**Vender:** That's right. I never forget. I always please my customers.

**Customer:** Another thing I like about this hot dog stand is that if you're in a hurry, this is the place to come because he is FAST.

**Vender:** That's right. I'm FAST. I always please my customers.

**Customer:** Hey, would you make me one of your big juicy hot dogs?

**Vender:** Sure. How would you like it?

**Customer:** Make it the same as you did last time, just as I always have it. *(Turns to audience)* He never forgets.

**Vender:** Oh yeah, I never forget.

**Customer:** And do it right away. I'm in a hurry.

**Vender:** Right. Just the same as last time and fast.

**Customer:** Say, I'm going to tell them *(Motioning to the audience)* exactly how I like my hot dog while you make it. Okay?

**Vender:** Okay. I won't listen. You just tell them. *(Vender leans over to listen while he prepares the hot dog.)*

**Customer:** He starts off with a long fresh baked hot dog bun, about this long. *(Shows with his hands)* He puts a fat juicy wiener cooked to perfection inside. *(Vender puts ingredients together as*

*Customer describes each item.)* Mmmm...I can smell it now. *(Vender starts to hand him the hot dog but Customer continues describing)* But what really makes it good is the mustard. You always have to have MUSTARD on a hot dog. Is that mine?

**Vender:** *(When Vender hears about the mustard, he stops before handling it to the Customer.)* No, this isn't yours. Yours has mustard, remember?

**Customer:** Yes. He never forgets.

**Vender:** I never forget. *(He puts mustard on the hot dog.)*

**Customer:** My hot dogs always have mustard...

**Vender:** *(Starts to hand hot dog to Customer)*

**Customer:** ...and CATSUP.

**Vender:** *(Quickly pulls back hot dog and adds catsup)*

**Customer:** *(Speaking to Vender)* You remember that I like catsup on my hot dog don't you?

**Vender:** Yes. I remember.

**Customer:** He never forgets.

**Vender:** I never forget. *(Starts to hand Customer the hot dog)*

**Customer:** The best tasting hot dogs have mustard and catsup...and ONIONS...

**Vender:** Onions? *(Pulls back hot dog to add onions)* Oh yes, onions go well with hot dogs.

**Customer:** Isn't he amazing? He never forgets.

**Vender:** I never forget. *(Starts to hand Customer hot dog)*

**Customer:** Yes, mustard, catsup, onions, and pickles.

**Vender:** Pickles? *(Pulls back hot dog to add pickles)*

**Customer:** *(To Vender)* Are you about finished?

**Vender:** Yes, I think so. *(Hands him the hot dog)*

**Customer:** Mmmm looks good, and you remembered everything! And you're fast too.

**Vender:** I remembered and I'm fast.

**Customer:** Thanks. *(Starts to eat the hot dog)*

**Vender:** Does it taste as good as you remembered?

**Customer:** Oh yes. It's delicious! *(Continues eating)*

**Vender:** That will be two dollars, please.

**Customer:** *(He looks at the hot dog and appears to be startled.)* What? I though you remembered?

**Vender:** Yes, I remember—you like mustard, catsup, onions, and pickles.

**Customer:** *(Continues to eat, ignoring Vender.)*

**Vender:** *(A little annoyed)* That will be two dollars.

**Customer:** But you said you remembered.

**Vender:** Yes, I remember.

**Customer:** *(Continues to eat, ignoring Vender)*

**Vender:** *(Getting mad)* That will be TWO DOLLARS!

**Customer:** Don't you remember?

**Vender:** *(Frustrated)* Remember what?

**Customer:** Remember that I don't have any money.

**Vender:** WHAT!

**Customer:** Now do you remember? *(Slowly backs away and quickly shoves the remainder of the hot dog into his mouth.)*

**Vender:** Yes, I do remember! And I'm FAST too.

**Customer:** Yikes! *(Jumps up in the air and comes down running.)*

**Vender:** I'm fast. I'll get you! *(Chases Customer off the stage.)*

The End

# I Want to Grow Tall

**Number of Participants:** Two

**Characters**: Short Man and Tall Man

**Costumes:** Street clothes

**Props:** None

**Setting:** A Short Man and a Tall Man are talking

## The Performance

**Short Man:** I want to grow tall.

**Tall Man:** Did you do what I told you to do?

**Short Man:** Yes, as you suggested I tried rubbing oil all over my body for a week, but it didn't work. In fact, I think I shrunk a half an inch. What's wrong?

**Tall Man:** What kind of oil did you use?

**Short Man:** Crisco.

**Tall Man:** Oh, no wonder. Crisco is shortening.

The End

# Judge Judith

**Number of Participants:** Seven

**Characters**: Judge Judith, Policeman, Young Man, Young Woman, Old Lady, Old Man, Drunk

**Props:** Six chairs and table (bench) for judge to sit behind.

**Setting:** Policeman is standing. Young Man, Young Woman, Old Lady, Old Man, and Drunk are sitting waiting their turn to come before the judge.

## The Performance

**Policeman:** Here yea, here yea, the Honorable Judge Judith presiding. Everyone rise.

**Judge:** *(Enters the courtroom and sits behind the table.)* Everyone be seated. The first case please.

**Policeman:** *(Escorts Young Man to front of the judge.)*

**Judge:** Young man, you have been brought in here for driving 80 miles an hour. What have you got to say for yourself?

**Young Man:** Judge, it's not true. I wasn't going 80. I wasn't going 60. I wasn't even going 40, or 30, or 20, or ten.

**Judge:** I'm fining you $50 for driving backwards on the street…Next case.

**Policeman:** *(Escorts Young Woman to front of Judge.)*

**Judge:** You are charged with going the wrong way on a one-way street. Didn't you see the arrow?

**Young Woman:** Arrow? Honest, Judge, I didn't even see the Indians.

**Judge:** It says here on your police report that you also made an inappropriate single. Officer, please explain.

**Policeman:** Yes, Your Honor. She put her hand out the window and signaled for a right turn, then she signaled for a left, then she moved her arm in a continuous circle.

**Judge:** What kind of signal is that?

**Young Woman:** I wanted to go right, then I change my mind and I wanted to go left. I changed my mind again, so I rubbed it out.

**Judge:** Women have a right to change their minds. Case dismissed. Next case.

**Policeman:** *(Escorts Old Lady and Old Man before the judge.)*

**Judge:** What are you here for?

**Old Lady:** I want a divorce.

**Judge:** You've got grounds?

**Old Lady:** Yeah, 81 acres north of town.

**Judge:** No, I mean, do you have a grudge?

**Old Lady:** Yeah, I've got a grudge on the farm—a two-car grudge.

**Judge:** How old are you?

**Old Lady:** Sixty-eight.

**Judge:** How old is your husband?

**Old Lady:** Seventy.

**Judge:** How long have you been married?

**Old Lady:** Forty-five years.

**Judge:** Why do you want a divorce?

**Old Lady:** Ah, enough is enough.

**Judge:** Explain.

**Old Lady:** He doesn't appreciate me and shows me no affection. *(Turns to husband)* Our neighbor Bob kisses his wife Mabel every morning. Why don't you do that?

**Old Man:** Why, I hardly know Mabel.

**Old Lady:** *(Disgusted)* Ooooh. I don't understand you. On Monday you say you like beans. Tuesday you say you like beans. Wednesday you say you like beans. Then all of a sudden on Thursday you say you don't like beans. You can't make up your mind.

**Old Man:** I was a fool to ever have married you.

**Old Woman:** I guess you were, but I was so in love with you at the time that I didn't notice…Judge would you like to be married to a man who doesn't come home at night and spends half the night drinking and gambling?

**Judge:** You have my deepest sympathy. He sounds like a miserable bum. *(To husband)* Is what your wife says true?

**Old Man:** *(Cupping hand to his ear)* What was that? I didn't hear you.

**Judge:** I said, is your wife honest? Can your wife tell a lie?

**Old Man:** You bet she can and she's real quick at it too. She can tell a lie as soon as it's out of my mouth.

**Judge:** The court shall grant this woman a divorce and 50 dollars a week alimony.

**Old Man:** (*Cupping hand to his ear*) That's very nice of you Judge. I'll even pitch in a few dollars myself.

**Judge:** Next case.

**Policeman:** *(Escorts drunk before the judge)*

**Policeman:** This man is here for drunk and disorderly conduct, Your Honor.

**Drunk:** Belch!

**Policeman:** How dare you belch before the judge!

**Drunk:** Oh, I'm sorry, I didn't know it was her turn.

**Judge:** My good man, you have been brought here for drinking.

**Drunk:** Hiccup! All right, Judge, let's get started.

**Judge:** *(To Policeman)* Where did you find him?

**Policeman:** Driving down Second and Main.

**Drunk:** But I wasn't driving. I was in the back seat.

**Judge:** Who was with him Officer?

**Policeman:** Nobody. He was driving from the back seat.

**Judge:** It seems to me that you have appeared before me in this court at least a dozen times in the last 20 years.

**Drunk:** Hiccup! I can't help it, Your Honor, that you're such a sorry judge that the Governor doesn't promote you to a higher court.

**Judge:** Take him to the tank.

**Drunk:** But Your Honor, I had only one drink.

**Judge:** From a glass or a bathtub?...Court adjourned.

The End

# The Lion Tamer

**Number of Participants:** Three

**Characters**: Stooge, First Man, Second Man

**Props:** Chair, whip, and rubber chicken. The chicken's legs are tied to a string and held up by a pole, like a fish dangling on the line of a fishing rod. The pole is propped up so the audience can clearly see the chicken.

**Setting:** First Man and Second Man walk by Stooge who is holding up a chair and cracking a whip at a rubber chicken dangling on the end of the line.

## The Performance

**First Man:** What's he doing?

**Second Man:** Practicing.

**First Man:** Practicing what?

**Second Man:** He wants to be a lion tamer.

**First Man:** But that's not a lion, it's a chicken!

**Second Man:** So's he. *(They continue to walk off the stage.)*

The End

# The Mind Reader

**Number of Participants:** Four

**Characters**: Swami, Manager, First Customer, Second Customer

**Costumes:** Swami wears a turban

**Props:** Blackboard, chalk, eraser, blindfold, can of red paint and paint brush, two chairs, and a table. Sign that reads "Swami the Magnificent—Mind Reader—Fortune Teller $5". Black hairy bug about the size of a tennis ball made from a ball of black yarn or cloth. Ten foot long, thin fishing line is attached to the bug, the opposite end of the line is a loop or hook.

**Set-up:** Swami conceals the black hairy bug up one of his sleeves, out of sight from the audience. The fishing line is thin enough that it is undetectable to the audience and can be placed on the tabletop. When Second Customer sits down at table, he will candidly attach the looped or hooked end of the line to his belt or coat during their conversation.

**Setting:** At the county fair or amusement park. Swami is seated at a table by a blackboard in the center of the stage. Manager, speaking like a sideshow barker, tries to entice customers.

## The Performance

**Manager:** See the Great Swami—he knows all, he sees all, he can reveal your future or answer your most troubling questions.

**First Customer:** Can he read minds?

**Manager:** Minding reading is one of Swami's specialties.

**First Customer:** How do I know he can really read minds?

**Manager:** He will demonstrate for you. He will put on this blindfold. You write any number on this blackboard and he will tell you what number it is.

**Swami:** *(Stands up and has blind fold put on)*

**First Customer:** Okay *(Goes over to the blackboard and writes the number three.)*

**Manager:** All right Swami what number did our friend write down. *(As he says this he slaps Swami's back three times.)*

**Swami:** You wrote the number "three."

**Manager:** See what did I tell you? This boy has a sick...er...a sixth sense.

**First Customer:** I don't know. Let me try it again.

**Manage:** Sure. Go ahead.

**First Customer:** *(Writes a zero on the board)* If you can get this one then I know you're on the level.

**Manage:** *(Baffled)* Ahh...

**First Customer:** Well, Swami what number is it?

**Swami:** *(Stalling)* Don't rush me, I'm concentrating, I'm concentrating...

**Manager:** *(Perks up because he just thought of an idea)* Swami will have it in no time. Right Swami? *(As he says this he kicks Swami in the seat of the pants.)*

**Swami:** *(Yells)* Oh! *(Takes off blindfold)*

**Manager:** There, he said "O." Didn't' I tell you he could do it?

**First Customer:** Okay then, if you can read my mind, what am I thinking?

**Swami:** You're thinking I can't read your mind.

**First Customer:** Mmmmm…Okay, here's five bucks tell me my future.

**Swami:** Oh, so you want me to foretell your future by reading your palm?

**First Customer:** Yeah, if that's how you do it. I want my palm read.

**Swami:** You want your palm read?

**First Customer:** That's what I said, I want my palm read.

**Swami:** Okay. *(He takes a paint brush with red paint and slaps it across his hand.)*

**First Customer:** Hey! *(Angry)* What are you doing?

**Swami:** You said you wanted your palm red.

**First Customer:** *(Slyly)* Ha, ha. Good joke. No hard Feelings. *(He extends his painted hand.)*

**Swami:** *(Grabs his hand to shake it)* Right, no hard feelings…Ohhhh. *(Looks at paint on his own hand)*

**First Customer:** So you can predict the future, you say. *(Looking skyward)* How are chances for a shower tonight?

**Swami:** It's okay with me, sir—take one if you need it!

**First Customer:** Listen, I've got a problem that you might be able to help me with.

**Swami:** What is it?

**First Customer:** The doctor told me I have a terminal disease and said I only have six months to live. What can I possibly do to live longer?

**Swami:** Here's what you do, go out and marry the ugliest, most ornery woman you can find.

**First Customer:** How on earth would that help?

**Swami:** Well, you may not live any longer, but I'll guarantee it will seem like the longest six months of your life.

**First Customer:** *(Smiles)* Oh, okay. Thanks. *(Exits)*

**Second Customer:** *(Enters)*

**Manager:** *(Begins calling for new customers)* The Great Swami—he knows all, he sees all, he can reveal your future or answer your most troubling questions. *(Addressing the Second Customer)* Do you have questions that you don't have answers to?

**Second Customer:** Yes.

**Manager:** Let Swami find the answers for you. Come right this way. *(Has Second Customer sit at the table)*

**Swami:** I will answer two questions for you for five dollars.

**Second Customer:** Don't you think five dollars is a lot of money for two questions?

**Swami:** Yes, it is. Now what is your second question?

**Second Customer:** Hey, wait a minute…

**Manager:** *(Breaks in)* For ten dollars Swami will answer all your questions.

**Second Customer:** Okay, here you go. *(Gives the Manager ten dollars)* I have a question that has been troubling me for years.

**Swami:** Yes, what is it?

**Second Customer:** You'll think I'm silly.

**Swami:** No, go ahead. No question is too silly.

**Second Customer:** No? You won't laugh?

**Swami:** No. What is your question?

**Second Customer:** What I want to know is: why is a watermelon filled with water?

**Swami:** *(Laughs)* Ha, ha…That's the dumbest question I've ever…

**Second Customer:** *(Upset)* Hey, you said you wouldn't laugh!

**Swami:** I know, but your question is so redicul…

**Second Customer:** Are you going to answer my question or not? Don't you know the answer?

**Manager:** *(Defensively)* Swami knows all the answers.

**Second Customer:** Nobody has ever been able to answer that question for me. It is like one of the unsolved mysterious of the universe. Why is a watermelon filled with water?

**Manager:** Go ahead and answer the man's question Swami. He's paid ten dollars. He deserves an answer.

**Swami:** *(Thinking)* Well…The answer is very simple. Ahh…A watermelon is filled with water…because…because it's planted in the spring!

**Second Customer:** Why of course! That makes so much sense. Perhaps you can answer *all* of my most puzzling questions?

**Swami:** Yes, I have all the answers. Fire away.

**Second Customer:** Where does a jellyfish get its jelly?

**Swami:** Ahh…from the ocean's currents.

**Second Customer:** Amazing! My next question: Can beer make me smart?

**Swami:** Well, it made Budweiser.

**Second Customer:** Incredible! Why do storks lift one leg?

**Swami:** If they lifted the other leg they'd fall over.

**Second Customer:** Unbelievable! What has six big eyes, eight legs, long fangs, and is very hairy?

**Swami:** *(Thinking)* Mmmm…Let's see…six big eyes, eight legs, fangs, hairy…ahh…Gee, I don't know…

**Second Customer:** *(Alarmed)* Me either but you got one crawling up your sleeve!

**Swami:** Yikes! (Screams, jumps up, reaches into his sleeve while dancing around hysterically, pulls out black hairy bug and throws it away towards Second Customer and runs off stage in the opposite direction.

**Manager:** *(Frightened, follows Swami)*

**Second Customer:** *(By this time Second Customer has already candidly attached the end of the fishing line to himself. As the bug is thrown toward him he screams hysterically, jumps and runs off the stage with the black hairy bug following as if chasing him.)*

The End

# Mr. Know-All

**Number of Participants:** Two (Can also be done with three if the third person is used for the radio voice.)

**Characters**: Mr. Know-All a telephone psychic, Caller, Radio Voice (optional)

**Costumes:** Mr. Know-all wears a turban.

**Props:** Two chairs, two small tables, two telephones, radio

**Setting:** Mr. Know-All is sitting in one chair by a table at one end of the stage and the caller is sitting in another chair by a table at the other end of the stage. Caller is listening to the radio as an advertisement for Mr. Know-All, telephone psychic, is broadcast. (The voice on the radio can be that of Mr. Know-All or a third participant.)

## The Performance

**Radio:** Do you have problems that are worrying you? Do you need answers to troubling questions? Are you having a difficult time with relationships, money, or family? If so, call Mr. Know-All, telephone psychic. He has the answer to all of your questions. He sees all, he hears all, he knows all. Call him today and he will answer your questions. The number to call is 555-5555.

**Caller:** Oh, that sounds great. I have a question that has bothered me for a long time. What was that number again?

**Radio:** The number is 555-5555.

**Caller:** Oh, yeah, right. (*Picks up telephone and dials number*)

**Mr. Know-All:** Hello. Mr. Know-All—Master Psychic, speaking. I see all, I hear all, I know all. How may I help you?

**Caller:** Hello. Do you know who this is?

**Mr. Know-All:** No, who is it?

**Caller:** It's me. Do you know why I'm calling?

**Mr. Know-All:** No, why?

**Caller:** To get some answers. Do you have the answers to all questions?

**Mr. Know-All:** Yes, I can answer all questions? I can see the past, the present, and the future.

**Caller:** Do you know what my question is?

**Mr. Know-All:** No, what is your question?

**Caller:** What did I have for lunch today?

**Mr. Know-All:** What! What type of question is that?

**Caller:** I'm testing you. I don't want to reveal to you personal information if you can't really help me.

**Mr. Know-All:** I can help you. Now tell me what is your question?

**Caller:** You sure you can see the past, the present, and the future?

**Mr. Know-All:** Yes, I can see everything, I know everything.

**Caller:** Well, how come you don't know what my question is?

**Mr. Know-All:** You haven't told me yet.

**Caller:** But it's personal.

**Mr. Know-All:** *(Leans forward with interest)* Oh, this sounds good. I won't tell a single soul.

**Caller:** No, it's too personal. If you're a real psychic you would know what my question is.

**Mr. Know-All:** I don't know the questions, I only know the answers.

**Caller:** Well then tell me the answer.

**Mr. Know-All:** But I need to know your question before I can give you the answer. So, tell me.

**Caller:** I can't. You should know what it is. If not, then you're just a fraud.

**Mr. Know-All:** All right. All right. Are you having financial problems?

**Caller:** No.

**Mr. Know-All:** You want to find your one true love?

**Caller:** No. I'm already married.

**Mr. Know-All:** You're having marital problems?

**Caller:** No, no, no!

**Mr. Know-All:** *(Looses patience)* WHAT IS YOUR QUESTION?!

**Caller:** If you crossed a cow with a kangaroo what would you get?

**Mr. Know-All:** (Shocked) What?! That's your question? What type of question is that?

**Caller:** It's just a test question. Before I trust you with my personal problem, I want to see how well you can answer a few simple questions first. So what's your answer? If you crossed a cow with a kangaroo what would you get?

**Mr. Know-All:** I'm not sure, but you're going to have to milk it on a pogo stick.

**Caller:** Okay, how about this one. How do Eskimos dress?

**Mr. Know-All:** As quickly as possible.

**Caller:** Why is the sky so high?

**Mr. Know-All:** So the birds don't bump their heads.

**Caller:** In this past Olympics who ran the 100-meter race the fastest?

**Mr. Know-All:** The winner.

**Caller:** *(Pleased)* Why, you DO have all the answers!

**Mr. Know-All:** I told you so. Now what is the question that has been troubling you?

**Caller:** Okay. I hope you can answer this one. I've always wanted to be famous. What can I do the get my name in lights?

**Mr. Know-All:** Oh that's easy, all you need to do is change your name to "Exit." Your name will be in lights everywhere.

**Caller:** Oh, thank you! That makes perfect sense. Good-bye.

**Mr. Know-All:** Good-bye. *(Hangs up phone and looks at audience)* That's why they call me Mr. Know-All.

The End

# My Name Is Not Melvin

**Number of Participants:** Four

**Characters**: First Man, Second Man, Third Man, Woman

**Costumes:** Street clothes

**Props:** Cigar, family photo, purse, baseball bat, and baseball hat.

**Setting:** Two men walk on stage from opposite directions. As they walk toward each other the First Man looks at the Second Man as if he recognizes him.

## The Performance

**First Man:** Well I'll be darned, if it isn't Melvin. How are you doing Melvin? *(Grabs Second Man's hand and shakes it like a long lost friend. He talks so fast the Second Man Hardly has time to say a word.)*

**Second Man:** *(Surprised and not knowing what to say because he doesn't recognize the man.)* Do I know yoоo…? *(His hand is being shaken with such vigor his whole body shakes as he says "you.")*

**First Man:** My goodness it's been a long time hasn't it? My good old friend Melvin. I haven't seen you in years. Say, how's that cute little sister of yours? You know I used to have a crush on her when we were kids. Is she married now? How's your folks? Gosh, this is just like old times. Here have a cigar. *(He pulls out a cigar while talking and shoves it into his friend's mouth.)*

**Second Man:** *(Looking totally confused and shakes his head no.)* Ahh…

**First Man:** Say, you're looking swell. I'd know you anywhere. You haven't changed a bit. Well…you have put on a little weight though haven't you? Looks like you've got a new suite too. Here have a light. *(Lights his cigar)*

**Second Man:** Ahh…I'm not...

**First Man:** My wife had another baby this year. That makes six. Let me show you a picture of my wife and kids. The kids have grown so much you wouldn't even recognize them. *(He shoves the picture into the man's hand.)* That's Jeffrey, Tommy, Bobby, Karen, Beth, Joanna, and, of course, my lovely little wife Sharon.

**Second Man:** They look nice, but…

**First Man:** How's your wife? Remember the time you and I were together on the beach at Miami and we saw her for the first time? You fell madly in love with her. *(Slaps him hard on the back)*

**Second Man:** Listen. I've never been to Miami. I'm not married. And my name is not Melvin. You've mistaken me for someone else.

**First Man:** *(Puts hands to his chest in astonishment)* What? You're not Melvin?...*(Becoming angry)* Why didn't you tell me you weren't Melvin? You could have told me you know. What kind of a guy are you? Do you do this sort of thing often? *(While he is talking he yanks the picture out of the man's hand and the cigar out of his mouth.)* I hope not. You should be ashamed of yourself. *(Starts to walk away, stops, turns around and kicks Second Man in the behind, the storms off the stage.)*

**Second Man:** Ouch! Hey…*(Watches man walk away, turns and begins to walk in the other direction.)*

**Woman:** *(Walks on stage toward Second Man. She recognizes him.)* Melvin? I've been looking all over for you. Where have you been? Don't tell me you've been at the tavern again.

**Second Man:** What?...ah. No…

**Woman:** *(Frowns)* I smell cigar smoke. Have you been smoking?

**Second Man:** No…well, er…Ah...yes…

**Woman:** *(Hits him with her purse)* How many times have I told you to stop smoking and drinking?

**Second Man:** Ouch…Hey!

**Woman:** How many times have I told you to quit your evil ways?

**Second Man:** Listen lady. I'm not who you think I am.

**Woman:** You're sure tootn' your not. You're nothing but a bum. *(She hits him again with her purse.)*

**Second Man:** Hey cut that out. What I mean is…I'm not Melvin.

**Woman:** What?

**Second Man:** I'm not Melvin. My name is…

**Woman:** You're not Melvin? Why are you going around pretending to be Melvin? You should be ashamed of yourself! *(She hits him with her purse and walks off.)*

**Third Man:** *(Walks on stage toward Second Man wearing a baseball hat and carrying a baseball bat. As he gets closer he stops and looks carefully at the Second Man. His eyes brighten up.)* Melvin! Is that you?

**Second Man:** *(Takes a step or two away)* No...

**Third Man:** Yes...MELVIN...my old buddy. *(Walks toward him.)*

**Second Man:** *(Backs up)* Oh...No. Not again. *(He turns and runs off the stage.)*

**Third Man:** Hey, Melvin! Wait up!*(Runs after him)*

The End

# The New Daddy

**Number of Participants:** Four

**Characters**: Mr. Brown, Mr. White, Mr. Green, Nurse

**Costumes:** Nurse wears distinctive outfit.

**Props:** Sign which reads "Grandview Hospital—Maternity Ward." Three chairs for the waiting room.

**Setting:** Three fathers-to-be are nervously pacing the waiting room floor as the Nurse comes in.

## The Performance

**Nurse:** Mr. Brown?

**Mr. Brown:** Yes?

**Nurse:** Congratulations, you're the father of twins!

**Mr. Brown:** Twins? Terrific! Hey, what a coincidence, I'm a player for the Minnesota Twins baseball team. *(Sits down relieved)*

**Nurse:** *(Leaves)*

**Mr. White and Mr. Green:** *(Nervously pace the room)*

**Nurse:** *(Enters)* Mr. White?

**Mr. White:** Yes?

**Nurse:** Congratulations, you're the father of triplets!

**Mr. White:** Triplets! Wow. What a coincidence. I work for the 3-M Company.

**Mr. Green:** Ohhh! *(Faints to the floor)*

**Nurse:** *(Kneels down to help him)* Mr. Green…Mr. Green…Mr. Green!

**Mr. Green:** *(Begins to come around)* Ohhh.

**Nurse:** Mr. Green. What's the matter?

**Mr. Green:** Quick, get me out of here.

**Nurse:** What for?

**Mr. Green:** I work for 7-11!

The End

# The Nightly News

**Number of Participants:** Five

**Characters**: Matt, Katie, Brent, Juan, Dr. Wortmore

**Costumes:** Matt, Katie, and Brent are dressed like TV news reporters.

**Props:** Table and chairs for Matt and Katie, microphones.

**Setting:** Matt and Katie are TV anchors hosting a news program.

## The Performance

**Matt:** Good evening and welcome to another edition of ABCD News Update. I'm your host Matt Lather and this is my co-anchor Katie Curie.

**Katie:** There's a lot happening in the world and local news today. In local news two priests from a monastery have opened a new gourmet fish and chips restaurant on Main Street...The owners are known as the fish friar and the chip monk.

**Matt:** A man from Pughbaugh, Kentucky was hurt badly last night when thrown from his horse...Doctors say he's in stable condition.

**Katie:** In the world of economics, while prices on most things continue to rise, paper products appear to be stationary...The latest market research shows that the price of duck feathers has risen dramatically over the past few months.

**Matt:** That's bad news, so now even down is up…Local crime seems to be on the rise as vandals put a hole in the fence to the nudist colony last night…Police are looking into it.

**Katie:** In an attempt to meet a growing need in the community the city board started an Apathy Support Group. Unfortunately the meetings were cancelled due to a lack of interest.

**Matt:** And in the medical field, a local resident claims to have discovered a new wonder drug. The only side effect is that when women take it, they feel compelled to join a convent. The FDA has refused to approve the drug. They say it's habit forming.

**Katie:** Today Mayor Sneezemore was taking a tour of an optician's office and accidentally backed into the lens grinding machine. Fortunately he was not seriously hurt.

**Matt:** Yes, but he did make a spectacle of himself.

**Katie:** In a bizarre coincidence, a butcher at Discount Meats had a similar experience as he inadvertently backed into his meat grinder.

**Matt:** I understand that nothing much happened except that he got a little behind in his orders.

**Katie:** That's right, but don't worry. They say they have plenty of ground rump roast for their sale this weekend.

**Matt:** Eleven tons of human hair was stolen from a doll factory in Central City this morning. Police are combing the area.

**Katie:** The first nationwide Janitorial Convention got underway this afternoon. Apparently they're calling for sweeping reforms.

**Matt:** George Juicy the CEO of Juicy Fruit Orange Juice Company retired today after 41 years on the job. The reason for retiring, he said, was because he just couldn't concentrate any more.

**Katie:** We now go to our man on the street Brent Breezeway. What do you have for us Brent?

**Brent:** It is a sad day for toad lovers Katie, as the lovable green amphibians were placed on the endangered species list. I have here noted toad psychologist Dr. Philpot Wortmore. *(Speaking to Dr. Wortmore)* Dr. Wortmore what are your thoughts about toads being put on the endangered species list?

**Dr. Wortmore:** This comes as no surprise to me, toads are always croaking.

**Brent:** You heard it here first on ABCD News. Back to you Katie.

**Katie:** A truck carrying copies of Roget's Thesaurus overturned on the highway this afternoon. Onlookers were stunned, overwhelmed, astonished, bewildered, and dumbfounded.

**Matt:** In national news, the president today slipped on his front porch and fell into his screen door. Fortunately, he wasn't hurt. He just strained himself.

**Katie:** We now go to our reporter on the street Brent Breezeway. Brent what have you got?

**Brent:** I have here with me internationally acclaimed physicist and best selling author Dr. ahh...ahh...what's your name again?

**Juan:** Toothree. It's pronounced "Too-three."

**Brent:** And your first name?

**Juan:** Juan.

**Brent:** That's right, Dr. Juan Toothree…Juan, I believe you said you had a twin brother?

**Juan:** Yes. His name is Ahmal

**Brent:** Could we meet him sometime?

**Juan:** Well, it's not really necessary. We're identical twins, so you know, you've seen Juan, you've seem Ahmal.

**Brent:** Ahh…right, Juan. I understand you've just written a new book on the theory antigravity.

**Juan:** Yes.

**Brent:** That's nice. Katie, back to you.

**Katie:** Matt have you read Dr. Toothree's new antigravity book?

**Matt:** You bet. I couldn't put it down!

**Katie:** In international news a freighter carrying a cargo of yo-yos was hit by an iceberg this afternoon. Apparently the ship sunk twenty-three times.

**Matt:** Incidentally, Katie, the captain of that ship did survive the wreckage, though he had to have his entire left side amputated! He's all *right* now.

**Katie:** In Paris today police arrested two teens, one who was drinking battery acid and the other eating fireworks. They charged one and let off the other.

**Matt:** An exciting discovery in the field of archaeology last week as a team uncovered the tomb where Napoleon and most of his family were buried. Unfortunately, they couldn't tell one bone apart from the another.

**Matt:** And in Bangkok, the world's first Silkworm Racetrack opened with a much hyped contest between two of the fastest silkworms around. Apparently the race ended up in a tie.

**Katie:** A tragic story out of Ireland where a plane crashed in the middle of a cemetery. So far rescue workers have uncovered 3,456 bodies.

**Matt:** Closer to home, notorious gangster Mugs Malone was released from prison today. He has vowed to change his life of crime and is opening up a chain of sausage delis… Talk about going from bad to wurst.

**Katie:** Farmers are extremely concerned about a new disease that affects dairy cows. It gives cows the urge to try to jump over barbed wire fences.

**Matt:** This could be an udder disaster!

**Katie:** Now let's go live to our on the spot reporter, Brent Breezeway. Brent What do you have for us?

**Brent:** *(Unaware he is live)* I've got a chili dog and a ham on rye, with pickles and…

**Katie:** *(Cutting in)* Ah, Brent we're on live TV. What have you got to report?

**Brent:** *(Embarrassed)* Ummmm…the weather here is dry. Back to you Katie.

**Katie:** *(Surprised)* What?...Ah…Let's see…*(Clears throat)* Ehem. A recent survey shows that 3 out of 4 people make up 75 percent of the population…What have you got Matt?

**Matt:** Er…And in other news, scientists are working around the clock. *(Turns to Katie signifying her turn to speak)* Katie.

**Katie:** That's our show for tonight. Remember, you heard it all here first on ABCD News. We bring you the latest news whether it's factual or not. Goodnight, Matt.

**Matt:** Goodnight, Katie.

The End

# The Novice Doctor

**Number of Participants:** Four

**Characters**: Doctor, Woman, Elderly Man, Younger Man

**Costumes:** Doctor wears white coat.

**Props:** Giant tongue depressor (measuring stick), small plastic frog, small mallet, large foam robber hammer, and a fake arrow through head.

**Setting:** The Woman is sitting in the Doctor's waiting room as the Elderly Man enters and sits down.

## The Performance

**Elderly Man:** Are you here to see the doctor?

**Woman:** Yes. He's so helpful.

**Elderly Man:** How's that?

**Woman:** Well, while most doctors just put a cast on a broken arm or leg, he does more. When I broke my leg, he showed me how to limp.

**Elderly Man:** Yes, he's very accommodating. He gave me six months to live. When I couldn't pay, he gave me another six months.

**Woman:** Isn't that sweet of him. My cousin Denny was so poor the Doctor allowed him to have his tonsils taken out one at a time. Poor luck though. When he couldn't pay for the second operation the doctor put the tonsils back in.

**Doctor:** *(Bursts into waiting room)* Call me a doctor—call me a doctor!

**Woman:** What's the matter, are you sick?

**Doctor:** No, I just graduated from medical school and I love being called "Doctor."…Are you here to see Dr. Fritzwilly?

**Man and Woman:** Yes.

**Doctor:** He's out sick today, so I'll be taking over for him while he's gone. Will you please come with me ma'am? *(They walk into the Doctor's office.)* Now, how may I help you?

**Woman:** *(Sneezes)* I've got a terrible cold. Can you do anything to help my sneezing? Ahh…choo!

**Doctor:** Yes, eat five cloves of garlic for breakfast, lunch, and dinner. Eat another five cloves just before you go to bed.

**Woman:** *(Surprised)* Will that cure my sneezing?

**Doctor:** No, but is will make you think twice before you sneeze.

**Woman:** Ahh…choo! What can I do to keep my head cold from going down to my chest?

**Doctor:** That's easy. Tie a knot in your neck…

**Woman:** *(Clears throat)* Ehem. I'm having difficulty speaking too. Something is wrong with my throat.

**Doctor:** Let's have a look. Say ahh.

**Woman:** Ahhhhhh.

**Doctor:** *(Pulls out two-foot long tongue depressor and tries to stick it down patient's throat. Patient struggles.)* Hold still...hold still...How am I going to find out what's wrong with you if you resist like this? Ah-haw...I see the problem. *(Pulls something out of the patient's throat)* You had a frog in your throat. *(He holds up a toy frog.)*

**Woman:** Oh, that feels a lot better. Thank you...Say, I also wanted to ask you about my son. He has a terrible nail-biting habit. How can I stop him from biting his nails all the time?

**Doctor:** Simple. Just have his teeth yanked out...

**Woman:** One more question. It's about my husband. He thinks he's a refrigerator.

**Doctor:** That's not so bad. It's a rather harmless complex.

**Woman:** Well, maybe, but he sleeps with his mouth open and the light keeps me awake.

**Doctor:** I sympathize with you. Did you know that your husband came to see me this morning?

**Woman:** He did! What's your prognosis?

**Doctor:** I hate to say this, but I don't like the way he looks.

**Woman:** Neither do I, but he's good to the kids.

**Doctor:** Well, that will be all for today.

**Woman:** Thank you Doctor. *(She leaves)*

**Doctor:** *(Speaking to Elderly Man in waiting room)* Come on into my office. *(They enter the office.)* How can I help you?

**Elderly Man:** Doc, I want you to look at my arm.

**Doctor:** *(He examines the arm and looks confused.)* What seems to be the matter with it?

**Elderly Man:** I have a stabbing pain in it.

**Doctor:** Hmmm…*(Opens a large medical book)* Is the pain near your elbow?

**Elderly Man:** *(Encouraged)* Yes.

**Doctor:** *(Looking at book)* Does the pain get worse at night?

**Elderly Man:** *(Getting excited)* Yes!

**Doctor:** *(Continuing to look at book)* Does it hurt when you move it?

**Elderly Man:** *(Anxious)* Yes, yes!

**Doctor:** Have you had this pain before?

**Elderly Man:** Yes.

**Doctor:** *(Slams the book closed)* Well, you've got it again.

**Elderly Man:** Isn't there anything you can do?

**Doctor:** Well, let's see... *(Picks up small mallet for testing reflexes)* I'm going to tap you with a hammer and you tell me if it hurts.

**Elderly Man:** Tap away Doctor.

**Doctor:** *(He gently taps patient's knee.)* Does that hurt?

**Elderly Man:** No.

**Doctor:** *(He stands to the side of the patient and gently taps his arm.)* Does that hurt?

**Elderly Man:** No.

**Doctor:** Okay, what about this *(Standing behind the patient he grabs a large foam rubber hammer and smashes it over the patient's head.)*

**Elderly Man:** Ouch!

**Doctor:** Well your reflexes are fine. You're as sound as a dollar. You'll live to be eighty.

**Elderly Man:** But Doctor, I am eighty.

**Doctor:** See, what did I tell you?

**Elderly Man:** But what about my arm?

**Doctor:** You say it hurts when you move it?

**Elderly Man:** Yes, that's right.

**Doctor:** Well then, don't move it.

**Elderly Man:** What?

**Doctor:** That will be all.

**Elderly Man:** Okay. *(Leaves)*

**Young Man:** *(Bursts into Doctor's office very frantic wearing fake arrow through his head.)* Doctor, Doctor, quick I've got to see you.

**Doctor:** *(Looks straight at Young Man with arrow poking out of his head.)* What seems to be your problem young man?

**Young Man:** I've got a splitting headache.

**Doctor:** *(Looks at him for a second)* Hmmmm…My advice to you is to take two aspirin and go to bed. If that doesn't work, go see a doctor.

**Young Man:** Thanks Doc. *(Leaves)*

**Doctor:** You're welcome. *(Looks at audience)* I love helping people.

The End

# The Operation

**Number of Participants:** Four

**Characters**: Dr. Von Scalpel, Dr. Liverpool, Nurse, Patient

**Costumes:** Doctors and Nurse dressed in surgical outfits. Patient dressed in hospital robe.

**Props:** Table or gurney, white sheets, toilet plunger, machete, large foam rubber hammer, red softball-sized ball, gasoline can, corn cob, rubber dog bone, 20 foot long rope, black wig, strapping tape, rubber snake, bag of chocolate chip cookies, and cooking tongs.

**Stage:** Operating room at hospital. The Patient is lying on the table. The sheets cover the table all the way to the floor. Props are hidden out of view from the audience behind the table.

**Setting:** Dr. Liverpool and Nurse are standing by patient who is lying motionless on the operating table. Dr. Von Scalpel, walks into the operating room holding freshly washed and sterilized hands up in front of him, palms facing him to keep them from touching anything. The Nurse stands behind the table near the foot. Dr. Liverpool is in the middle and Dr. Von Scalpel walks behind the table at the head.

## The Performance

**Dr. Von Scalpel**: Is this the patient Dr. Liverpool?

**Dr. Liverpool:** Yes, Dr. Von Scalpel.

**Dr. Von Scalpel:** *(Looking at Patient)* Fold the sheet down. I have to keep my hands sterile for the operation.

136

**Dr. Liverpool:** *(Folds top sheet over toward the audience)* Yes sir.

**Dr. Von Scalpel:** *(Fighting from sneezing)*
Ahh…ahh…ahhhh…ahhhhhhhhhhhhhhh…*(Sneeze builds up to a climax than abruptly disappears with a faint sigh.)* Phew… *(suddenly)*…AHH-CHOOOOO! *(Sneezes all over his freshly washed hands. He wipes his sleeve and hands across his nose. Looks for something to wipe his hands off on, finding nothing wipes his hands on his pants.)* Are you ready Dr. Liverpool?

**Dr. Liverpool:** Yes sir.

**Dr. Von Scalpel:** Hand me the scalpel.

**Dr. Liverpool:** *(Turns to Nurse)* Scalpel.

**Nurse:** *(Hands Dr. Liverpool a machete)* Scalpel.

**Dr. Liverpool:** *(Hands the machete to Dr. Von Scalpel)* Scalpel.

**Dr. Von Scalpel:** Is this thing sharp?

**Dr. Liverpool:** *(Shrugs his shoulders)* I don't know.

**Dr. Von Scalpel:** I need something to test it on. *(Looks from side to side)* Ah, I'll use a hair. *(Grabs a strand of hair on the Patient's head and plucks it off)*

**Patient:** Ouch! *(Screams, but remains lying motionless)*

**Dr. Von Scalpel:** *(Startled, looks at Patient to make sure he's been anesthetized, then continues to test the machete by splitting the hair.)* It's sharp enough. *(He begins to cut the*

137

*patient open by gently poking him in the chest with the end of the machete.)*

**Patient:** Ouch! *(Remains motionless)*

**Dr. Von Scalpel:** *(Startled, draws back, looks at sleeping patient and tries again.)*

**Patient:** Ouch!

**Dr. Von Scalpel:** *(Becoming annoyed)* What's this? *(Looks closely at sleeping patient and jabs him several times with the machete.)*

**Patient:** Ouch, ouch, ouch, ouch! HEY! *(Sits up)* That thing is sharp!

**Dr. Von Scalpel:** *(Shocked, drops knife then looks at Dr. Liverpool)* Dr. Liverpool did you anesthetize the patient?

**Dr. Liverpool:** *(Turns to nurse)* Nurse did you anesthetize the patient?

**Nurse:** No. I thought you did.

**Dr. Liverpool:** *(Speaking to Dr. Von Scalpel)* No, we thought you did.

**Dr. Von Scalpel:** *(Quickly)* Anesthetic!

**Dr. Liverpool:** *(Turns to nurse)* Anesthetic!

**Nurse:** *(Picks up empty gasoline can with the words "Anesthetic" written on it and hands it to Dr. Liverpool.)* Anesthetic.

**Dr. Liverpool:** *(Hands gasoline can to Dr. Von Scalpel)* Anesthetic.

**Dr. Von Scalpel:** *(Grabs the can and whacks Patient over the head with it.)*

**Patient:** Ohhh…*(Collapses back onto the table.)*

**Dr. Von Scalpel:** There that will keep him under for awhile. *(Picks up knife, wipes it off on his sleeve and begins cutting Patient open. He starts up near the Patient's shoulder and saws, pulls, and struggles with the knife cutting all the way down the Patient's body to the end of his foot.)* There, that ought to do it.

**Dr. Liverpool and Nurse:** *(Nod their heads in agreement.)*

**Dr. Von Scalpel:** *(Looks into the incision and extends his hand toward Dr. Liverpool.)* Forceps.

**Dr. Liverpool:** *(Turns to Nurse)* Forceps.

**Nurse:** *(Hands Dr. Liverpool a large pair of cooking tongs)* Forceps.

**Dr. Liverpool:** *(Hands the tongs to Dr. Von Scalpel)* Forceps.

**Dr. Von Scalpel:** *(Takes the forceps and begins roaming around inside Patient)* Ah-haa…*(Pulls out a large red ball)* I got it. *(Holds the ball with forceps so audience can clearly see)*

**Dr. Liverpool:** What is it?

**Dr. Von Scalpel:** It's a blood clot. Here get rid of it.

**Dr. Liverpool:** Okay. *(Grabs the clot with his hand, looks side to side. Finding no place to put it he tosses it behind his back.)*

**Patient:** *(As soon as the clot hits the back wall or floor, he yells.)* Ouch!

**Doctors:** *(Look startled. They look closely at the Patient as he lies motionless, then shrug their shoulder and continue.)*

**Dr. Von Scalpel:** *(Looking inside the Patient)* He's got something else in here. Looks like a blockage in his stomach. Hand me the stomach pump.

**Dr. Liverpool:** *(To Nurse)* Stomach pump.

**Nurse:** *(Grabs toilet plunger and hands it to Dr. Liverpool)* Stomach pump.

**Dr. Liverpool:** *(Passes pump to Dr. Von Scalpel)* Stomach pump.

**Dr. Von Scalpel:** Here we go. *(Takes plunger and places it on Patient's chest and begins pumping)*

**Patient:** *(As the doctor pushes down on the plunger Patient's arms and legs rise and fall. This is repeated several times.)*

**Dr. Von Scalpel:** I think it's loosened up. *(He looks curiously inside the Patient.)*

**Dr. Liverpool:** What is it Doctor?

**Dr. Von Scalpel:** I don't know. *(He reaches into Patient's stomach cavity and pulls out a bag of cookies.)* What did this patient have for lunch?

140

**Dr. Liverpool:** It's a bag of chocolate chips cookies! *(Grabs the cookies out of Dr. Von Scalpel's hand)* Let me see that. *(He opens the bag and eats a cookie and shares them with the other two.)* Mmmmm.

**Dr. Von Scalpel:** *(Eating cookie)* Not bad…

**Patient:** Oooh…oooh. *(Sits up)* I don't feel so good.

**Dr. Von Scalpel:** *(Yells)* ANESTHETIC! Quick!

**Dr. Liverpool:** *(Passes the gasoline can to Dr. Von Scalpel)* Here.

**Dr. Von Scalpel:** *(Grabs the can and belts Patient over the head)*

**Patient:** Ohhh…*(Drops back down unconscious)*

**Dr. Von Scalpel:** *(Relieved)* They don't make anesthetic like they used to. *(He takes a drink from the gas can, like it was a jug of moonshine and hands it back to Dr. Liverpool and looks back inside the Patient.)* Let's see what do we have here? *(Startled)* Something moved!

**Dr. Liverpool:** What is it Dr. Von Scalpel?

**Dr. Von Scalpel:** I think it's a tapeworm. *(He reaches in and screams)* Ouch! *(He pulls his hand out of Patient's incision with a rubber snake biting his finger.)* It won't let go. Hurry, get me a hammer!

**Nurse:** Hammer. *(Hands very large foam rubber hammer to Dr. Liverpool)*

**Dr. Liverpool:** Hold still. *(Furiously starts hitting the worm as well as Dr. Von Scalpel's hand, arm, and head)*

**Dr. Von Scalpel:** Ouch…Oh…Ahh. *(Grabs worm with his other hand and pulls it off his finger, throws it to the floor and stomps on it)* Take that!

**Doctors:** *(They all calmly go back to the operation as if nothing happened.)*

**Dr. Von Scalpel:** Mmmmm, what's this?

**Patient:** Hee, hee. *(Giggles and squirms slightly but remains lying on table)*

**Dr. Von Scalpel:** *(Stops. Looks at Patient who is now silent and motionless, scratches his head perplexed. Shrugs shoulders and reaches back inside.)*

**Patient:** Hee, hee. *(Again squirms and giggles even louder)*

**Dr. Von Scalpel:** *(Stops and looks at Patient who is motionless again)* Let's continue. *(Reaches back in)*

**Patient:** Ha, ha, hee, hee, haaa. (Bursts out in uncontrollable giggles and laughter)

**Dr. Liverpool:** What's happening?

**Dr. Von Scalpel:** Nothing. I just found his funny bone. *(He pulls out a rubber doggie bone.)*

**Patient:** Ha, ha…*(Sits up laughing hysterically)*

**Dr. Von Scalpel:** *(Quickly grabs the gasoline can and hits him over the head with it.)*

**Patient:** Ohhh… *(Falls back down)*

**Dr. Von Scalpel:** *(Takes another drink)*

**Dr. Liverpool:** *(Pointing into Patient's incision)* Dr. Von Scalpel, look at that?

**Dr. Von Scalpel:** *(He looks and reaches in and begins pulling out the end of a piece of rope.)* This is his intestine. We ought to get rid of some of this, he's got way too much and I can't see a thing in here. *(He begins pulling it out. It keeps coming and coming and coming. After pulling out about 20 feet of rope it stops as if caught on something. He pulls harder. It doesn't come. Concealed from view, Patient holds the end of rope to give the appearance it is caught on something.)* Dr. Liverpool it's stuck. Give me a hand. *(They both pull and struggle sometimes even pulling against each other.)* Stop! Let's do this together. On the count of three we will pull together.

**Dr. Liverpool:** Okay.

**Dr. Von Scalpel:** One, two, three! *(They pull and the end of the rope flies up out of the patient. On the end of the rope is a black wig. The doctors see it and scream and drop the rope.)*

**Dr. Liverpool:** What is it?

**Dr. Von Scalpel:** *(Picks up the rope and dangles the wig in the air)* Why, it's merely a hair ball.

**Dr. Liverpool:** Say Doctor, what's this patient's problem anyway?

**Dr. Von Scalpel:** What?

**Dr. Liverpool:** I mean, why are we operating on him?

**Dr. Von Scalpel:** *(Dumbfounded, scratches his head)* Ahh…Nurse, what's wrong with this man?

**Nurse:** Why doctor didn't you know? He has a pain in his big toe.

**Dr. Von Scalpel:** Is that all?

**Nurse:** Yes. He wanted you to take a look at it.

**Dr. Von Scalpel:** Let me look at his foot. *(Examines Patient's toes)* I see the problem. *(He grabs the machete and smacks it down on the table like he's cutting something off the patient's foot.)* He had a corn growing on his toe. *(Holds up a cob of corn)*

**Dr. Liverpool:** What's the patient going to do when he finds out what we did to him simply to remove a corn?

**Dr. Von Scalpel:** *(Thinking)* Hmmmm.

**Patient:** *(Starting to slowly come around)* Ohhhhhh…

**Dr. Von Scalpel:** Hurry, gather all this stuff up and we'll put it back before he comes to. *(They all quickly rush around gathering up everything that was removed from the patient, including the corncob, snake, and blood clot, and stuff it back inside him.)*

**Nurse:** Hurry, he's coming around.

**Dr. Von Scalpel:** *(After everything is back inside the patient, he grabs some strapping tape and puts several strips of tape* *across the patient's chest to close the incision and one large strip from shoulder to toe.)*

**Patient:** Ohhh...I feel funny. *(Sits up with tape all over him)* Why is my stomach so upset? What happened? What's all this tape for?

**Dr. Liverpool:** The surgery was a success. You're as good as new.

**Patient:** Surgery? What surgery?

**Dr. Von Scalpel:** Ahh...Didn't you come in to get a corn removed?

**Patient:** No, I came in for an examination. Why does my head hurt?

**Dr. Von Scalpel:** Ahhh...Here take a drink of this, it will help you feel better. *(Hands him the gasoline can)*

**Patient:** This looks familiar. *(Angry)* Hey, I remember now. You're the guy who keeps hitting me over the head with this thing.

**Dr. Von Scalpel:** *(Nervous, he starts to slowly back away)* Well...you didn't want us to operate without anesthesia did you?

**Patient:** *(Very angry)* Operate! You operated on me!

**Dr. Von Scalpel:** Oops!

**Patient:** Why I'll clobber you! *(Raising the can above his head he leaps off the table and chases the others out of the room.)*

The End

# The Operation II

**Number of Participants:** Four

**Characters**: Dr. Von Scalpel, Dr. Liverpool, Nurse, Patient

**Costumes:** Doctors and Nurse dressed in medical attire. Patient has bandages over his face.

**Props:** Bed or gurney for Patient

**Setting:** Recovery room at hospital. The Patient is lying in bed. Dr. Liverpool and Nurse enter and look down at hospital bed.

## The Performance

**Dr. Liverpool:** She looks pretty good, eh?

**Nurse:** *(Surprised)* What?

**Dr. Liverpool:** I said, the patient looks good, doesn't she?

**Nurse:** Did you perform plastic surgery on this patient?

**Dr. Liverpool:** Why yes. What's the matter?

**Nurse:** You numbskull…the woman who was in for plastic surgery is in room 66B. This is room 3!

**Dr. Liverpool:** Oh, no! *(They both look down at the patient in shock)* Well, uh…do you think *he'll* like it?

**Dr. Von Scalpel:** *(Enters the patient's room)* Well, well, how is my patient?

**Dr. Liverpool and Nurse:** *(Surprised)* Your patient?

**Dr. Von Scalpel:** Yes, my patient. I just removed her left leg.

**Nurse:** Dr. Von Scalpel, this is *Mr.* Spudly.

**Dr. Von Scalpel:** *(Shocked)* Mr. Spudly! Isn't this room 99 47?

**Nurse:** No, Dr. Von Scalpel. This is room 3.

**Dr. Von Scalpel:** Oh, my gosh! I always get these rooms mixed up.

**Dr. Liverpool:** Me too. I thought it was room 66B and gave Mr. Spudly, a face lift, tummy tuck, and breast enlargement.

**Dr. Von Scalpel:** *(Remorseful)* Oh, no! How could we have been so stupid! *(Crying)*

**Dr. Liverpool:** *(Holding back tears of anguish)* Yes, stupid, stupid, stupid. I'll never forgive myself.

**Nurse:** Doctors, you've got to stop blaming yourselves.

**Dr. Liverpool:** *(Thinks for a second, then perks up)* Okay. Let's go get some lunch.

**Dr. Von Scalpel:** *(Smiles)* Sounds good to me.

**Nurse:** Me too. *(They all leave for lunch.)*

The End

# A Picnic at the Park

**Number of Participants:** Three

**Characters**: Boy, Girl, Fly

**Costumes:** Street clothes

**Props:** Two large colorful cloth napkins or handkerchiefs, two plastic forks, two plates, two plastic knifes, two paper plates, two white paper napkins, a large bag of peanut M&M candies, a fly swatter, an old pump-type bug sprayer (empty), a rubber mallet, a small whisk broom, a bottle of catsup, salt and pepper shakers, and a large brown paper bag.

**Setting:** This skit is done in pantomime. The voice for fly is the only one that makes a sound and remains off stage during the entire skit.

## The Performance ▬▬▬▬▬▬▬▬▬▬▬▬▬

Boy and Girl carrying a paper bag walk on stage. They look around searching for a good spot for a picnic. Boy walks to center of stage and motions Girl to follow him. He gestures to this spot. She makes an "okay" sign with her fingers and they both smile. She begins to sit down and he holds out his hand signaling to "stop." He reaches into his coat or back pocket and pulls out a whisk broom and sweeps the spot clean. He then motions for her to sit down. They sit down at a slight angle to each other but still facing the audience.

Girl reaches into the bag and removes a cloth napkin, shakes it open, and places it in front of Boy. He helps flatten all the corners and makes sure it smooth and flat. Girl removes a second cloth

148

napkin and lays it in front of her. They both smile at each other and look pleased.

Girl removes a paper plate from the bag and places it in the center of Boy's napkin. She places another paper plate on her napkin. She proceeds to remove the plasticware and paper napkins and place them next to the plates. The Boy smiles and occasionally looks at the audience.

Girl removes the salt, pepper, and catsup and puts them on the Boy's napkin. The setting is fit for an elegant lunch. But instead of anything fancy, she pulls out the bag of M&M candies and places a few on Boy's plate and a few on her own plate then replaces the bag of candy into the grocery bag.

At this point a voice offstage makes a buzzing sound like a fly. The Girl looks up and follows the flight of the fly by moving her head around in a wavy motion and then looks straight down in front of them. The Boy points his finger at the fly, almost touching it. The Girl removes a fly swatter from the bag and swings it down hard on the fly, hitting Boy's finger. He grimaces in pain. Voice from offstage makes buzzing sound as fly takes to the air and buzzes around them. Girl swings swatter this way and that trying to hit the fly in the air. As she swings the swatter haphazardly around, she accidentally hits Boy. He flinches in pain. She signals that she's sorry. The buzzing stops.

They settle down and continue to eat lunch when the voice off stage begins buzzing again. Girl lifts the swatter as if to start swinging it around again and Boy frantically singles "No!" She puts the swatter down, reaches into the paper bag and pulls out the bug spray and begins frantically spraying everywhere, including the Boy's face. The buzzing noise stops. He looks sick and faints. Shocked to see him fall over, she stops and make sure he is okay.

He comes around and they continue to eat lunch. Using their forks and knives they try to eat the M&Ms, but the candies keep falling back onto their plates before they can get them into their mouths. They become frustrated. Girl motions that she has an idea and tells Boy to put down his plasticware. She reaches into the paper bag and with one sweep, pulls out a rubber mallet and very quickly begins smashing the M&Ms on both plates. This action must be done very quickly to create the humor. The mallet is then quickly returned to the bag. Boy stares at plate in amazement.

Both now begin to eat the smashed candies but stop, and look up. They hold up the palms of their hands indicating that it is raining. Quickly, they grab their cloth napkins, letting their plates and candy fall to the floor, drape the napkins over their heads, and run off the stage out of the rain.

The End

# The Portrait

**Number of Participants:** Two

**Characters**: Artist and Customer

**Props:** Easel, stool, sign, and paint brushes.

**Set-up:** The easel and stool are set up with a sign that reads: "Your Portrait Painted for $10." The Easel is facing away from audience so they can't see what is being painted.

**Setting:** Artist is on stage waiting for business. Customer enters stage and reads sign. The skit can be done entirely in pantomime.

## The Performance

The Customer indicates that he wants his portrait painted and pays the artist. The Customer is directed to sit on the stool in front of the easel. The artist begins painting his portrait. He uses a variety of strokes. Some actions require wide arm movements like he is splashing paint all over the canvas and at other times he is close-up doing fine detail. Often be backs away from the canvas, tightens his left hand into a fist with his thumb sticking straight up and held at arm's length as if taking a careful measurement then continues painting. He uses different brushes including a 4-inch paint brush and a roller. The Customer stands up and the Artist turns the canvas around so everyone can see his masterpiece. The painting is a picture of the artist's thumb. Angry the Customer grabs the canvas lifts it high over his head as if to hit the Artist, and chases him off the stage.

The End

# Ouch!

**Number of Participants:** Two

**Characters**: Small Man and Big Man

**Costumes:** Exercise clothes

**Props:** Large foam rubber hammer, paper money, lightweight barbells, one #260 balloon (the type used to make balloon animals), chest expander with springs, a stack of paper money, a large funnel, and a jug of water.

**Setting:** Two men are working out in a gym.

## The Performance

*(Big Man is lifting a set of heavy-looking weights with ease. Small man picks up the chest expander and tries to stretch it out, but has difficulty. He struggles without success. He gets an idea. He reaches into his pocket and pulls out a deflated #260 balloon. He tries to stretch it out like the chest expander, but has difficulty and struggles. As he is struggling he inches closer to the Big Man who has his weights lifted high over his head. One end of the balloon slips out of the Small Man's hand and snaps the Big Man in his ribs. He yells, drops the bar onto his head and winches in pain. Then drops the weights on his foot and yells again. Sound effects from offstage can help as the weightlifter is struck each time.)*

**Big Man:** *(Angry)* Hey! What's the big idea? I ought to knock you silly. *(Stepping closer to clobber Small Man)*

152

**Small Man:** *(Scared but putting on bluff)* Oh, yeah? You better not tangle with me if you know what's good for ya.

**Big Man:** *(Skeptical)* Yeah, why's that?

**Small Man:** I'm stronger than Tarzan.

**Big Man:** No, you're not

**Small Man:** Yes, I am

**Big Man:** How do you know?

**Small Man:** I can beat my chest without hollering.

**Big Man:** I think I'll knock your block off.

**Small Man:** Wait! You don't recognize me? I'm Rocky Knockout, a professional boxer.

**Big Man:** Never heard of you. When was the last time you were in a fight?

**Small Man:** I was in one last night.

**Big Man:** Who with?

**Small Man:** My wife…She came crawling to me on her knees.

**Big Man:** Yeah? What'd she say?

**Small Man:** Come out from under that bed, you coward.

**Big Man:** Last fight I was in I broke a guy's nose in two places.

**Small Man:** Well you won't do that to me.

**Big Man:** Why not?

**Small Man:** I don't plan on going anywhere near those to places.

**Big Man:** You think you're tough don't you wise guy? Look at these muscles. *(He shows off his muscles.)*

**Small Man:** Oh, yeah. Well, look at these muscles. *(He flexes his muscles, but nothing happens)* Just a minute, they were around here somewhere. *(He flexes his right bicep and with his left hand candidly pushes the muscle up to make it look bigger.)*

**Big Man:** I don't think you're so tough. I bet you $10 you can't make me say "ouch." *(Pulls out a 10 dollar bill and places it on the floor)*

**Small Man:** Oh, yeah. I bet you $100 you can't make me say "ouch." *(Pulls out several bills and places them on the floor)*

**Big Man:** Oh, you think you're so confident. I bet you $1000 you can't make me say "ouch." *(Pulls out a handful of bills and adds it to the pile)*

**Small Man:** You only want to bet $1000! What's the matter? You chicken? I'll bet you a million dollars you can't make me say "ouch." *(Pulls out of his pockets a stack of money and tosses it on the pile)*

**Big Man:** *(Becoming mad)* Okay, you're on. *(Removes wads of cash from his pockets and adds it to the pile)* To show you how tough I am I'll let you go first.

**Small Man:** All right. This will be a quick bet. *(Small Man pulls out a large foam rubber sludge hammer. Chuckles because he thinks he will easily win. He hits Large Man over the head. Offstage a bell is struck as the hammer hits his head. The Large Man stands there smiling like nothing happened.)*

**Large Man:** Haw! Is that it? Okay now it's my turn. *(Grabs Small Man's nose between the knuckles of his first and second fingers and gives a sharp twist.)*

**Small Man:** *(Winches in pain as his nose is being twisted and almost falls to the ground. He grabs his mouth to keep himself from yelling "ouch" although some audible squeals are heard.)*

**Large Man:** Ha, ha. This is fun. Take your turn.

**Small Man:** Would you mind if you closed your eyes.

**Big Man:** Okay. But it won't help you.

**Small Man:** *(He walks up to Big Man looks him over. He practices a few punches to the Big Man's stomach then winds up and lets him have it. Offstage a drum bangs at the same time. The Big Man stands still and smiles.)*

**Big Man:** Are you finished yet?

**Small Man:** No, not yet. Keep your eyes closed. *(He grabs a large funnel)* Here hold this. *(The end of the funnel is placed inside the front of the Big Man's trousers. He grabs a jug of water and dumps it into the funnel.)*

**Big Man:** *(Startled)* Woo! Enough. I'm through playing around with you. It's my turn and you're going to get it now. *(Grabs Small Man around the neck and begins to choke him)*

**Small Man:** Stop! No more. Stop! Take the money.

**Big Man:** *(He lets the Small Man go.)* This was a piece of cake. *(As he bends over to pick up the money the Small Man kicks him in the seat of the pants or for a louder effect, he may use a slapstick. The Big Man jumps into the air.)* OUCH!

**Small Man:** You said "ouch." I won! *(Quickly gathers up the money while Big Man looks on dumbfounded, then chases Small Man with his arms loaded with money off the stage.)*

The End

# Quick-Draw

**Number of Participants:** Two

**Characters**: Quick-Draw Machine and Stooge

**Costumes:** Cowboy outfit for quick-draw machine.

**Props:** Two toy guns (one of which is a water pistol), small box, sign which reads "Beat the Fastest Draw in the West. Only 25 cents."

**Setting:** Mechanical cowboy on the stage wearing a water pistol. Stooge enters. Reads sign.

## The Performance

**Machine:** Quick-draw contest. Try your luck and see if you can beat the fastest draw in the West. Only 25 cents. Quick-draw contest. Only 25 cents.

**Stooge:** I bet I can beat that stupid machine. *(Steps up to the machine and deposits a coin in the Machine's front shirt pocket)*

**Machine:** Ding! *(Rocks gently back and forth to indicate that it is turned on)* Welcome to the quick-draw contest. Remove the gun from the box. Turn around, and as I count, walk three paces, turn and fire. May the best man win.

**Stooge:** *(Removes gun from the box turns around and starts to walk as machine counts)*

**Machine:** One…two…*(Just as Stooge makes the third step, Machine points the water pistol and shoots him on the back of the head with a stream of water)* Three! Bang! Bang! You're dad. You lost.

**Stooge:** *(Surprised)* Hey! You cheated!

**Machine:** *(Game is over)* Quick-draw contest. Try your luck and see if you can beat the fastest draw in the West. Only 25 cents. Quick-draw contest. Only 25 cents.

**Stooge:** I'll try it again. This time I'll only take two steps. No dumb machine is going to beat me. *(Deposits coin)*

**Machine:** Ding! Welcome to the quick-draw contest. Turn around, and as I count, walk three paces, turn and fire. May the best man win.

**Stooge:** *(Gets into position, giggles as if he is going to get the upper hand on the machine this time)*

**Machine:** One…*(Just as Stooge takes a second step the machine squirts him in the back of the head with his water pistol.)* Two, three. Bang! Bang! You're dead. You lost. Quick-draw contest. Only 25 cents. Quick-draw contest. Only 25 cents.

**Stooge:** *(Upset)* Okay, cowboy. I'm going to get you this time. No dumb machine is going to bet me. I'll turn on the count of "one" this time. *(Deposits coin)*

**Machine:** Ding! Welcome to the quick-draw contest. Turn around, and as I count, walk three paces, turn and fire. May the best man win.

**Stooge:** *(Gets in position and giggles as if he is going to win)*

**Machine:** *(Points gun at the back of Stooge's head before counting)* One…

**Stooge:** *(Quickly turns around and is immediately squirted in the face)* Hey!...I'll get him this time! *(Deposits another coin and steps back facing the machine with his gun pointed at its face)*

**Machine:** Ding! Welcome to the quick-draw contest. Turn around, and as I count, walk three paces, *(Speech begins to slow down)* t-u-r-n…a-n-d…*(Stops as if the battery has run down)*

**Stooge:** *(Frustrated and lowers gun)* Drat! No power.

**Machine:** *(Quickly points gun at Stooge and shoots him in the face)* Bang! Bang! You're dead. You lost.

**Stooge:** *(Very angry)* Why you! *(Points gun at machine as if to shoot)*

**Machine:** STOP! *(Points)* Look behind you. *(As Stooge turns to look, Machine starts to tip-toe away)*

**Stooge:** There's nothing there *(Turns and sees Machine trying to sneak away)* Hey, come back here! *(Chases him off the stage)*

The End

# The Radio

**Number of Participants:** Four or more

**Characters**: Boy, Girl, Dr. Humdinger, Radio (Two or more characters can play the part of the Radio.)

**Costumes:** Street clothes

**Props:** Two chairs, a table, and a radio.

**Setting:** Boy and Girl enter room. Radio is resting on table.

## The Performance

**Boy:** Do you want to watch TV?

**Girl:** No, there's nothing good on tonight.

**Boy:** Why don't we listen to the radio. There's always something interesting on the radio.

**Girl:** Okay.

**Radio:** Click... *(Advertisement)* Don't ruin your hands washing dishes with ordinary dish detergent use Scrubo instead...Yes, my friends, Scrubo is so powerful it will clean the dirt right out from under your fingernails. Your dishes will never look so clean.

**Girl:** Find something good on.

**Boy:** Okay.

**Radio:** Click… *(Singing in a horrible high-pitched voice)* Tiptoe to the window, by the window, that is where I'll be, come tiptoe through the tulips with me…

**Boy and Girl:** *(Disgusted)* Ohhhh.

**Radio:** Click. This is station KKOP bringing you the best in… Click…earwax removal. Yes, Flush Away will wash out that nasty… Click…neighbor next door who always comes over… Click…with heartburn and acid indigestion. So when you need fast relief…Click…use Drano. Use it once and your pipes will stay clean for weeks. If you act now we will also give you a free… Click… *(Talk Show)*…spinal tap and if that doesn't work Doctor Dinkel, what would you do next?...Click… *(Singing)*…Tiptoe from the garden, by the garden of the willow tree and tiptoe through the… Click… *(News)*…snake infested jungles of East Africa. Rebels fought to keep… Click…the square dance tradition alive. Country western singer Hank Horseshoe said that he prefers…Click…Avon deep red lipstick, because of it's smooth creamy texture and sensuous yet… Click…nutty taste which makes it the most popular breakfast for kids. Next time you're at the grocery store ask for…Click…stinky socks and dirty towels—they all come out smelling clean and fresh when you use… Click…Gastro motor oil. It cleans and lubricates like no other oil can. When you want your motor to run smooth, reach for the best, reach for…Click…Dr. Hinkel's Toe Gel. For fast relief of athlete's foot no other medication comes close. Just one dab will make you… Click… *(Singing)*… Tiptoe through the tulips with me… Click... *(News)*… Stop! Don't touch that dial. This late breaking news just in. A swarm of killer bees have crossed the US-Mexican border and are headed straight for Los Angeles. In response, authorities there have called out the S.W.A.T. team…Its news like this that gets the whole city buzzing. We have here with us Dr. Albert Humdinger an expert on bees. Dr. Humdinger why do you think these killer bills are flying to Los Angeles?

**Dr. Humdinger:** Well, it's faster than walking.

**Radio:** You heard it here first on Radio KLOP. Now for the weather. Warning! We have a tornado headed this way. This is the type of storm where you want to keep your mouth closed because it looks like a real tongue twister.

**Girl:** What else is on?

**Radio:** Click…Today our special guest is the internationally famous mime Marcel Mooso. Thank you for being on our program today. What's it like being a mime?… *(Silence)*…Hmm, I *see*… And how did you handle this situation?… *(Silence)*… I *see* what you mean…And then what happened?…*(Silence)*… I *see* your point… What happened when they asked you to sing the national anthem?… *(Silence)*… Yes, I would have been speechless too. What did you think about the president's speech?… *(Silence)*… Oh, I *see* you don't have too much to say about that. I don't blame you, it's mostly double-talk anyway. Thank you, Marcel, for that wonderful interview. We will now be talking calls from our listeners. If you have a question for Marcel, give us a call at 555…

**Girl:** Change the station.

**Radio:** Click…Does your breath stink?

**Boy:** *(Startled)* What?

**Radio:** I said, does your breath stink? Do you have bad breath?

**Boy:** I dooo no…

**Radio:** Do your friends avoid you because your morning breath could choke a rabid dog? If so, you need Stink-Away the new all-mouth breath freshenizer. Unlike other mouthwashes, Stink-Away penetrates deep within your gums and throat sanitizing and sterilizing everything in its path. Stink-Away is the only mouthwash made with Clorox bleach, which has been proven in clinical tests to kill germs on contact. Stink-Away must be good because four out of five Dental Assistants surveyed say they might even try it. Before going out on the town, use Stink-Away and your date won't be frightened away by monster breath. Sold at dental and janitorial supply stores everywhere. Get yours today...Now back to the program. Here we are back to radio KKOK were we play all your favorites. Speaking of favorites, here is one of my all time favorite songs...*(Singing)*... Tiptoe through the tulips, through the garden, through the...

**Girl:** STOP! Turn it off.

**Boy:** Let's watch TV. There's a new comedy show on right now.

**Girl:** I know, but it's a joke.

**Boy:** Your favorite police show got canceled.

**Girl:** Yeah, I think it's a crime.

**Boy:** Hey, let's go to a movie. Do you like sad movies?

**Girl:** For crying out loud, no.

**Boy:** Hey, there's a new vampire movie playing. Do you want to go watch it?

**Girl:** Yeah, I hear it's a real scream. *(They both hurry off to the moves.)*

The End

# The Restaurant

**Number of Participants:** Two

**Characters:** Waitress and Customer

**Costumes:** Waitress wears an apron

**Props:** A chair and table

**Setting:** The Customer is sitting at a table in a restaurant.

## The Performance

**Waitress:** *(Serves Customer a meal)* Here you are sir.

**Customer:** Thank you. This sure looks good.

**Waitress:** Enjoy your meal.

**Customer:** Thanks. I will. *(He takes a bite and bursts into uncontrollable laughter.)*

**Waitress:** *(While walking away she hears Customer laughing and turns around and looks at him for a moment. When Customer stops laughing she shrugs her shoulders and begins to walk away.)*

**Customer:** *(He takes another bite of food and cracks up laughing hysterically.)*

**Waitress:** *(Looks at Customer again, scratches her head looking puzzled than goes about her business as the laughter dies down to a mere giggle.)*

**Customer:** *(Takes another bite of food and again bursts out laughing even louder and longer than before.)*

**Waitress:** *(Looks at Customer again. This time getting a bit annoyed and curious. She walks up the Customer.)* Is there something wrong sir?

**Customer:** Yeah, this food…It tastes funny! *(Customer runs off the stage with the Waitress chasing him.)*

The End

# Robbing Hood

**Number of Participants:** Two

**Characters**: Masked Man and Poor Man

**Costumes:** Poor Man is dressed in shabby clothes

**Props:** Mask for Masked Man, pistol, and a stack of stage money.

**Setting:** Two men walk on stage from opposite ends.

## The Performance

**Masked Man:** You sir!

**Poor Man:** Who me?

**Masked Man:** Yes you. Have you got any money?

**Poor Man:** Why no. I don't have a penny to my name.

**Masked Man:** Well this is your lucky day.

**Poor Man:** *(Curious)* It is?

**Masked Man:** Yes. *(He pulls out a stack of money and hands it to the man.)* Here's five thousand dollars.

**Poor Man:** *(Shocked)* Wa…What's this for?

**Masked Man:** I steal from the rich and give to the poor.

**Poor Man:** *(Smiles and becomes excited)* Yahoo! I'm rich! Rich, rich, rich!

**Masked Man:** *(Pulls out a gun and points it at the Poor Man)* All right—stick 'em up!

**Poor Man:** What?

**Masked Man:** I steal from the rich and give to the poor. *(He takes the money and quickly exits)*

**Poor Man:** *(Looks bewildered)*

The End

# The Telephone Conversation

**Number of Participants:** Two

**Characters**: First Man and Second Man

**Props:** Telephone

**Setting:** Two friends are talking as phone rings.

## The Performance

**First Man:** *(Answering phone)* Hello…*(Turns to Second Man)* It's Barney.

**Second Man:** *(Nods acknowledgingly)*

**First Man:** *(Continues conversation on phone)* What was that Barney?…*(Surprised)* You don't say!…Wow…*(Stunned)* You don't say!….Incredible…*(Shocked)* You don't say! Okay, good-bye.

**Second Man:** *(Anxious)* What did he say?

**First Man:** I don't know. He didn't say.

The End

# This Old Man

**Number of Participants:** Two

**Characters**: First Man and Second Man

**Costumes:** Street clothes

**Props:** None

**Setting:** Two slightly hearing impaired old men meet on the street.

## The Performance

**First Man:** Hello, Joe.

**Second Man:** Hi, Sam. What's new?

**First Man:** *(Cupping his hand and putting it up to his ear)* Eh? What did you say?

**Second Man:** *(Raising his voice)* I said, what's new?

**First Man:** Oh, Fine, thanks.

**Second Man:** Windy, isn't it?

**First Man:** Eh?

**Second Man:** *(Raising his voice)* I said, windy, isn't it?

**First Man:** No, it Thursday.

**Second Man:** What was that?

**First Man:** *(Raising his voice)* It's Thursday.

**Second Man:** So am I, let's go and have a cup of coffee. *(Both exit to get coffee)*

The End

# A Tramp Down the Street

**Number of Participants:** Two

**Characters**: Tramp and Man

**Costumes:** Tramp is dressed in shabby cloths. Man is wearing street clothes and a sweater.

**Props:** A paper dollar

**Setting:** Man is walking down street when a Tramp approaches him to ask for a handout. He sticks out upturned hat, but Man walks on by. Tramp follows after him.

## The Performance

**Tramp:** Mister, would you give me five dollars for a sandwich?

**Man:** I don't know. Let's see the sandwich.

**Tramp:** Mister, I haven't tasted food for a week.

**Man:** *(Trying to ignore him)* Don't worry, it still tastes the same.

**Tramp:** Wait, don't go. *(Secretly sticks his hand in the Man's pocket)* You wouldn't want me to starve would you?

**Man:** What are you doing with your hand in my pocket?

**Tramp:** I want a match.

**Man:** Why don't you ask for it?

171

**Tramp:** I don't talk to strangers.

**Man:** Me either and you're definitely strange. *(Starts to walk away)*

**Tramp:** Could you spare five dollars…how about four dollars?

**Man:** You remind me of my wife.

**Tramp:** How's that?

**Man:** My wife is always asking for money. Last week she wanted $200. The day before yesterday she asked me for $150. This morning she wanted $100.

**Tramp:** That's crazy. What does she do with it all?

**Man:** I don't know. I never give her any.

**Tramp:** I'm not surprised.

**Man:** I don't come down here often. Are you familiar with this part of town?

**Tramp:** Sure, I'm here every day.

**Man:** Well, I'm in a hurry. Could you tell me the quickest way to the Bank Building?

**Tramp:** Sure, run as fast as you can…Could you spare two dollars?

**Man:** Why don't you get a job?

**Tramp:** No one will hire me.

**Man:** Why not? Do you have a criminal record?

**Tramp:** I got caught for stealing a calendar once.

**Man:** And what did you get?

**Tramp:** Twelve months.

**Man:** I've got to run.

**Tramp:** Wait. *(Grabs hold of Man's sweater)*

**Man:** Hey, don't harm my sweater. Do you know how many sheep it takes to make one sweater?

**Tramp:** No, I didn't even know they could knit…How about one dollar?

**Man:** I'm in a hurry.

**Tramp:** Why don't you take a taxi? There's one right over there.

**Man:** He's the one who brought me here. He's a terrible driver—he nearly killed me twice.

**Tramp:** Don't be too hard on him. Give him one more chance.

**Man:** I've got to go.

**Tramp:** What's your hurry?

**Man:** I own a shoe store and I'm checking out a new line of shoes.

**Tramp:** A business owner, eh? Say, would you give me a job?

**Man:** I'm sorry, I can't. I just haven't got enough work to keep you busy.

**Tramp:** I think you'd be surprised at how little it takes to keep me busy.

**Man:** No, I'm sorry.

**Tramp:** Well how about that dollar?

**Man:** Okay, I'll give you a dollar. *(Hands Tramp a dollar)*

**Tramp:** No thanks, forget it. I don't work that cheap.

The End

# The Trapeze Act

**Number of Participants:** Four or more

**Characters**: First Man, Second Man, three or more clowns

**Costumes:** First and Second Man wear street clothes, clowns wear clown costumes

**Props:** None

**Setting:** First Man and Second Man walk by a group of clowns and stop. The clowns are looking up at the ceiling as if observing something swaying back and forth high above them.

## The Performance

**First Man:** What are they doing?

**Second Man:** Watching the trapeze act.

**First Man:** *(Goes over to the group and looks up, then comes back)* There's nothing up there.

**Second Man:** I know.

**First Man:** You know! Then what are they looking at?

**Second Man:** They're rehearsing.

The End

# Tug-of-War

**Number of Participants:** Four

**Characters**: Strongman and three stage hands.

**Props:** A long rope.

**Stage:** The stage must have wings or curtains on each side.

**Setting:** This skit is done in pantomime, although the strongman may add grunts and groans or other appropriate sound effects. Strongman enters the stage pulling on a rope.

## The Performance

The Strongman struggles and pulls while slowly inching his way across the stage. It appears he is battling a group of men or perhaps a team of horses pulling on the other end. The other end is out of sight from the audience and is held by a stage hand. The struggle continues. Sometimes the Strongman is pulled back but he fights to regain lost ground. He slips and is pulled back but quickly gets back up. Finally he pulls the rope all the way across the stage. As soon as he is out of sight of the audience he hands the rope to the second and third stage hands. The stage hands keep the rope tight across the stage keeping the seesawing motion going as if the struggle is ongoing. Meanwhile, the Strongman runs around backstage to the other side of the stage. Here he takes the rope from the first stage hand and continues the struggle. He slowly enters the stage tugging on the rope making it appear as if he is pulling against himself. Two stage hands hold the other end of the rope. Halfway across the stage the Strongman falls down facing forward and is quickly dragged off. Two stage hands are needed to pull the Strongman quickly off the stage.

The End

Printed in Great Britain
by Amazon.co.uk, Ltd.,
Marston Gate.